BOUNDLESS

CHAUNTÉ LOWE

SCHOLASTIC
FOCUS
NEW YORK

Library of Congress Cataloging-in-Publication Data

Names: Lowe, Chaunté, 1984– author.
Title: Boundless / Chaunté Lowe.
Description: First edition. | New York, NY : Scholastic Focus, 2023. | Audience: Ages 8–12 | Audience: Grades 4–6 | Summary: "Everything seemed set against Chaunté Lowe. Growing up with a single mother in Paso Robles, California, where she experienced food insecurity, homelessness, and domestic abuse, Chaunté couldn't imagine a future that offered a different sort of life. But then, one day, she turned on the TV and there was Flo Jo, competing in the Olympics and shattering records in track and field. Almost immediately, Chaunté knew what she wanted to do. She started running. With the help of a small community of friends, family, and coaches, Chaunté worked as hard as she could — both in the classroom and out on the sports field — and through her own fierce determination and grit, she overcame every imaginable obstacle, eventually propelling herself to the place she always dreamed about: the Olympic medal podium. Boundless is a story that will move anyone who's ever had a big dream, ever dared to hope for a better future, and ever believed that nothing was impossible. In her own words, Chaunté presents her remarkable and inspiring story of loss and survival, perseverance and hope"— Provided by publisher.
Identifiers: LCCN 2022016417 | ISBN 9781338741520 (hardcover) | ISBN 9781338741537 (ebook)
Subjects: LCSH: Lowe, Chaunté, 1984-—Juvenile literature. | African American women track and field athletes—Biography—Juvenile literature. | Olympic athletes—United States—Biography—Juvenile literature. | Jumping—United States—Juvenile literature. | BISAC: JUVENILE NONFICTION / Biography & Autobiography / Sports & Recreation | JUVENILE NONFICTION / Family / General (see also headings under Social Topics)
Classification: LCC GV1073.15.L68 A3 2023 | DDC 796.43/2092 [B]—dc23/eng/20220521
LC record available at https://lccn.loc.gov/2022016417

10 9 8 7 6 5 4 3 2 1   23 24 25 26 27

Printed in Italy   183

First edition, March 2023

Book design by Keirsten Geise

This book is dedicated to the many people who helped raise me. It takes a village to raise a child, and my village is the reason why I am who I am today.

To my family, who has supported me in every endeavor and let me know my life was worth fighting for.

Finally, this book is for the child who is feeling hopeless. Remember, the life that you are living today does not have to be the life that you live when you grow up. Do not give up on your dream. Keep going! Your future is worth fighting for.

Never forget that the most beautiful rainbows always come after the most horrific storms.

1

THE EYES OF MY HEART

As FAR AS I could tell, it was going to be another hot summer afternoon spent hanging upside down, feet perched against the back of our brown corduroy couch and my head dangling inches from the floor. Typically, as a child with untreated ADHD, I had enough energy to play for every hour that the sun danced across the blue sky. However, today was grocery day. Grocery day was the worst day of the week because our family didn't own a car, which meant we had to walk everywhere.

"Chaunté, put on your shoes," my mother called from the small, dimly lit kitchen. Unpleasant memories of our long, exhausting caravans immediately flooded my mind.

"Do I have to?" I pouted. I could practically taste the dry, hot air that only intensified with each car that whooshed past us as we trekked along the slightly raised concrete path, the pink soles of my shoes ripping away from their white, glittered bodies.

My mother walked into my room, stooped down, and tied my tattered high-tops. Trying to make the best of this crummy situation, she said, "Well, how about this? I'll get you some new shoes when I can, but for now, let's pretend these old sneakers are new sandals."

I marveled at her ability to artfully play my emotions like a fine-tuned instrument. She knew I loved to imagine, and she exploited this fact to get me peacefully out the door. Feeling empowered by my newfound ability to choose my perspective, I stopped to admire my new "sandals" and skipped happily outside.

My mother, my two older sisters, and I would walk the three and a half miles to the store, shop for about an hour, and then walk the three and a half miles back. From the oldest to the youngest, we were all expected to do our part and carry two bags of groceries on the trip back. These walks were painful. My little arms shook as I continuously repositioned my fingertips inside the handle loops of the plastic bags. Every few yards, the sweat of my palms would force me to set my bags down, dry my hands on my pants, and reset my grip. Powering through the pain with my head down, I read the paved trail beneath me, "Rock, crack, dried piece of gum." We'd walked this path so many times that I'd memorized the scars of the sidewalk like the lines of my favorite Dr. Seuss book.

The whole adventure took several hours, and by the end of it, I was exhausted. Unenthused by the blistering California sun, I opted to spend the rest of my day inside, watching the spectacle of my sisters fighting over which TV channel we should watch. Being the youngest of three sisters, I offered no opinion and sat safely outside the lines of this battlefield. Leaving them to squabble, I let my mind wander and imagined what it would be like if I could travel beyond the borders of this sleepy town. Paso Robles, California, was nineteen point five square miles of mostly oak trees, vineyards, and farmland. With our feet being our only mode of transportation, I'd walked what seemed to be every square inch of it. Desperate to see more, I often badgered my relatives with questions about faraway places without ever getting a satisfying answer. Limited by finances and fear, no one in my family had ever been outside the state of California. These barriers were so crippling that we rarely ventured more than thirty miles away from our secluded hometown.

The fight between my sisters must have escalated rapidly, because my mother swooped in, settling the argument by choosing the channel herself. If I'd had a choice, I would have chosen the news. Channel 6 was my passport around the world, giving me glimpses into lands that I was sure I would never set foot on.

When I watched our wooden-boxed television, it was like the glass screen that I gazed into held the power to open a vast world full of endless possibilities and wonder. Each show had its own ability to take my glazed eyeballs beyond the confinement of whatever four walls I was stuck inside, into a limitless oasis of hope and promise. It's incredible how many hours I spent watching my television until I found "It." "It" being the substance of what my curiosity was continually searching for. It's the thing that would eventually prove to be the element that anchored me to this earth. The one thing that jumped off the screen to spark something in my heart and firmly plant my feet on a path that took me toward my destiny. That moment came in the summer of 1988.

I was four years old, and I was watching the Olympics for the very first time. With a slim and pointy frame, I was lying on my stomach on the living room floor, my elbows planted deep in dark shag carpet, my chin resting in the palms of my hands as my feet swung up and down in utter delight.

For weeks I had heard everyone talking about the Games, but nothing could have prepared me for what was about to take place. The glowing light of our two-dial television jumped off the screen, and that's when I saw her. "FloJo," whose real name was Florence Griffith Joyner, emerged from the depths of a long dark hallway, heroically taking her place on the South Korean coliseum track.

The warmth of Seoul's summer sun prompted sweat beads to gather just above her focused brows. Her piercing eyes glared down the steaming red track, laser-focused on the prize before her. Unbothered by the throngs of wildly cheering fans who flailed and bellowed behind her, Ms. Joyner took her place behind her starting blocks. Not realizing this moment was the calm before the storm, I took the opportunity to study her. Her hair was a lengthy mane, thick and wafting in the wind. Her nails, perfectly manicured, were long and painted patriotically to match her Team USA uniform. Everything about her screamed femininity, but her strength was undeniable. With the number 569 displayed on the bib pinned to her red top, the intensity in her posture let me know she was waiting for something to happen. Then, the starter, who stood on top of a short ladder off to the side of the track, raised a gun into the air. Gripping a mic with the other hand, he yelled, "Runners, to your mark."

The once thunderous crowd now hushed in anticipation and hung on his every word. Instinctively, the Olympian moved forward and placed her feet into the starting blocks.

"Get SET."

Her flawless nails digging into the track, the human bullet readied herself in the runner's position—

POW! The gun sounded.

FloJo shifted the weight through her hands, majestically converting that strength into power as her feet thrust hard against the stationary blocks. The resistance of this action forcefully jolted her body from the starting line, propelling her into the race of her life.

When the gun sounded, each of the eight runners seemed to be evenly matched across the expanse of the track. Open hands, high knees, and tipped toes pressed into the red-lined rubber. Each of their steps powerfully struck the ground repeatedly, accompanied perfectly by the look of determination in each woman's eyes. Without knowing the context of what was going on, one could still understand that the stakes were high. For some reason, my eyes kept returning to FloJo.

Graceful as a gazelle but with the strength of a roaring lion, she overtook each of her opponents one by one. Like a fiery dart, she crossed the line first, breaking the Olympic record with a time of 10.54 seconds over 100 meters. Ripping me out of that moment, a screeching yelp assaulted my ears from behind me. It was my mother.

Jumping up and down joyfully, she exclaimed, "I knew she could do it!"

Her excitement puzzled me. How did my mom know this woman? To my surprise, her sentiment echoed beyond our walls. Through the open window of our living room, I could hear shouts of celebratory cheers coming from every open window and doorway of our apartment complex. That was the moment when I realized that what was happening was more significant than just a race around a track. The Olympics was a force that crossed geographic, cultural, and socioeconomic barriers, bringing people together all across the world.

I was hooked. With the Olympic torch of my heart now lit, I knew what I wanted to do with the rest of my life. I could no longer contain the inner excitement that erupted inside me. I blurted out at the top of my lungs, "I WANT TO BE AN OLYMPIAN!"

Thinking that there was no better time than the present, I began to run around our small two-bedroom apartment, crashing into the furniture, emulating my newfound "Shero." After several close calls with our delicate glass lamps, my mother told my older sister and me to go outside.

Seizing the opportunity to have my mom's full attention, I asked, "Mom, what would it take to become an Olympian? I want to be just like this FloJo woman."

My mother told me it would take hard work and perseverance. Unimpressed, partly because it sounded difficult and mostly because I didn't know what those words meant,

I scoured the room for a second opinion. My eyes locked on to the second-wisest person I knew: my older sister, who was six years old.

Desperate for a quick solution to the burning question, I repeated the question to my sister. "What would it take to become an Olympian?" I asked.

Pausing for a moment, with her arms crossed and her fingers rubbing her chin, my sister aimed her eyes up at the sky and responded, "You know what can make you run faster? Eating dirt."

Having nothing to lose and only being four years old at the time, I felt this advice was reasonable. Not wanting to waste a single moment, I exclaimed, "Let's go!"

We hurried down the wooden staircase to a very unusual place to play. The complex parking lot was the closest thing I had ever seen to a track, and to me, it was perfect. Cars lined the center of the lot inwardly facing one another. This design created an oval-shaped concrete loop that bumped up against the various apartment buildings. Separating the two lines of cars was a row of berry bushes planted in a patch of the "treasure" I was searching for.

Without hesitation, I filled my fingertips with the dry earthy dirt and dropped it into my mouth. Ignoring the taste and without chewing, I swallowed it. I looked to my sister for approval, but instead, she laughed at me. "Haha! You fell for it," she chuckled.

For the first time, I was unbothered by one of her pranks because, at that moment, I believed that it had worked. Immediately from within I felt faster, stronger, and more able to achieve this giant-size goal.

Picturing myself in a crowded stadium with wildly cheering fans, I took my place. I stood behind the white line painted on the black concrete positioned in an empty parking space and said, "Runners, to your marks." I crouched down, one knee on the ground, and got into my imaginary blocks.

"Get set." I pressed my dirt-tinged fingernails into the ground.

"GO!" I imagined the bang of the gun signaling me on toward victory. I ran around the parking lot as fast as I could. Feeling like I was flying, I ran faster than I had ever run before, with the wind hitting my face and the summer sun beating on my back.

From that moment, I knew my life would never be the same. I continued like this the entire summer. Every day, climbing down the stairs, lining up at my mark, and running as fast as I could around the concrete oval. When I lay in bed at night, I would recall the historic 100-meter race, where the most heroic woman I had ever seen placed her feet in the blocks and won the heart of the world. I didn't know when my time would come, but I knew that when it did, I would be ready.

2

GRANDMA SURPRISE

As THE SCORCH of the sun dimmed, the rich hues of deep red and radiant orange of the leaves signaled that summer was coming to an end. Like a relay race with smooth transitions, the baton of time ushered us from the searing summer heat of August into the autumn breezes of September. Just like the seasons, a lot had changed in my life in a relatively short amount of time. One change was a big move that would alter my life forever. Exchanging our cramped apartment for a two-story townhome allowed us to experience a lifestyle that was foreign to us yet exciting. My mother had just completed a work training program that qualified her for steady income with a new career. Now working at a chiropractor's office as an assistant, we were able to afford many things that we couldn't before.

Living in this pristine building lined with pomegranate and apricot trees gave me a sense of pride that I had never had in my home. Many times, I couldn't believe we were able to call this place home, but my fear of being ripped away from my parking lot track workouts was a real concern for me. Thankfully my fears were unfounded and short-lived because we were now within walking distance of the city's largest park. After school, once my homework was completed, I waited for my mom to come home from work. Still without a car, the convenience of a ten-minute walk to Dr. Myers Chiropractic ensured that my mom would always make it home shortly after leaving the office. Like clock-work, at 5:10 p.m. my mom strutted around the corner, bag in hand, heading down the sidewalk toward our door. As I peeked out the window my heart raced with excitement, anticipating my favorite part of the day. Track practice! After a light jingle of her keys, the lock softly grinded before the doorknob turned on its face to smile at me sideways. As it swung open, the door let out a gentle whine, signaling that it was finally time to go.

As soon as she opened the door, I stretched out my arms and jumped into her embrace. Squeezing her neck tightly, I leaned in and kissed her cheek. Arching backward to get a better look at her face, I stared deeply into her eyes and said, "Are you ready to go yet?"

Giggling, she said, "All right, little girl, hold your horses." Examining me from the top of my head to the soles of my shoes, she performed a mental readiness checklist before pointing at my feet. "Okay, please double knot your shoes. We don't want you to trip over your laces and fall again." She was right. I was always so busy trying to be as fast as I could that I often fell, tripping over my shoelaces. Stooping down first to my left foot and then my right, I grabbed the bunny ears of the silver-speckled laces of my new high-tops. Satisfied with the secure knots my little fingers formed, I stood straight up and stamped the soles of my new hole-free shoes squarely on the ground. Upon contact, the lights on the sides and heel of each shoe blinked on.

Joined by my sisters, our walk to the park was brisk and uneventful. Delighted to finally be clear of whooshing cars, I slid my hand from my mom's tight grip and darted across the grass, through the thick sand, and straight to the merry-go-round. The merry-go-round was a green steel-framed octagon with enough seating for twenty or so kids. The steel structure was anchored in the center by a tall pole that allowed the ride to spin, powered by the legs of strong-willed children.

Merry-go-round "code" was that certain kids would get assigned as pushers while others were allowed to hang on, remain seated, and enjoy the ride. There was an unwritten rule that the littlest kids never had to push because their legs didn't move fast enough, and they would get dragged in the sand or end up flying in the air and hanging on for dear life. The exception to this rule was me. I had built a reputation for being the fastest and strongest kid who ever visited the Paso Robles City Park. Most kids didn't like to push because pushing meant that you didn't get to enjoy the ride. I, on the other hand, loved pushing, motivated by my goal to reach the Olympics.

I knew that the medals would go to the fastest runners when the time came, but I also knew that it would be difficult to be faster than every other person in the entire world. I had no way of measuring if I was getting faster, but that didn't stop me from trying. One day when I volunteered to be a pusher, I accidentally discovered that running against the weight of the spinning steel and the resistance of the sand inadvertently caused my body to run significantly faster when I returned to a flat, solid surface. I could feel my legs moving with less effort and at a speed that made it feel like my feet were churning like a spinning wheel. To me this was gold. In my five-year-old mind, I concluded that the more I could do this the faster I could become. So now I always volunteered to push, and adopted it as my preferred form of training.

After a long day's work, we headed home, hungry and exhausted, for dinner. Macaroni and cheese, fried chicken, and homemade biscuits with jam were on the menu. My mom and my sister Tania cooked as my other sister, Alexis, and I set the table. Sitting around the square table with the glass top, we prayed to give thanks and ate. One by one Mom asked us about our day as we told her stories of math, reading, and science. Wanting to update her on my athletic progress, I decided to also tell her about PE.

"So today they made us run around the entire playground. They said it wasn't a race, but I know it's always a race. When the teacher said go, I took off faster than everyone else and beat everyone by a lot. At the end of the lap, I stayed there and cheered for the other kids and told them good job when they finished. When PE was over, the teacher told me that she thinks I may be the fastest person in my entire grade, and I think she may be right. I wonder if they will let me race the next grade to see if I'm the fastest in that grade too."

Delighted, my mom listened to me and smiled as she finished her meal.

With a new home came new responsibilities. At the beginning of the week, we were given a list of chores and if they were all completed by the end of the week, we would get allowance. One of our chores was washing the dishes.

Implementing weekly chores was a way for my mom to empower us to learn the relationship between hard work and earning money. Once the money was earned it was ours to keep or spend however we chose.

Tonight was our night to clear the table and wash the dishes. Completely unenthused and utterly disgusted, I pretended to gag while lined up at the sink flanked by my sisters. I groaned when I lost the third round of Rock, Paper, Scissors, knowing I would be assigned food duty. Food duty was the absolute worst part of doing dishes. Getting allowance hinged on me touching everyone else's leftover food.

"Eww," I softly whined. "I think Alexis should do this because she's better at it than me."

"Ha ha, not a chance," she chimed in smugly, knowing that the outcome of Rock, Paper, Scissors was written in stone and this nasty job was all mine.

Unable to see through the soapy suds, I plunged my hands deep into the lukewarm water. I felt bits of macaroni touching my forearm, which caused my skin to itch. Rebelling against this grotesque task, I blurted out, "I'm not doing this," as I withdrew my arm from the murky sink.

"Come on, Chaunté! You have to be a team player," Alexis said.

Then Tania chimed in, "Don't you know if one of us doesn't do our chores then none of us will get our allowance? You can do it. Just find a way to get through it." I knew they were right. I already had plans for my allowance. I had recently fallen in love with candy and had my heart set on getting a king-size bag of Skittles.

I was surprised at how their encouragement helped me to will my way through an unpleasant task. I'm not sure if it was my mom's plan all along, but working together as a team pushed us to do something we didn't think we could do. One plate after another, I plunged my hand deep into the sink, scrubbed the dishes with the soapy rag, and handed them to Alexis to rinse off and dry. Time flew as we each did our part to contribute to our team. Once finished, Tania summoned my mom to examine our work, and we were awarded our allowance.

Giddy with excitement, we danced around the kitchen, our money in hand. Overjoyed by this playful mood, I turned to Alexis, and, with the most serious expression I could muster, I said, "Hey, Lex, do you want my money?"

Confused but not wanting to miss any opportunity, she reached out for my dollar, saying, "Yes I do."

Before she could grab it, I snatched my hand back in a hurried motion and said, "You snooze you lose. You can't touch this," while giggling and hopping around with a joyful heart.

Trailing away in laughter, we turned off the kitchen lights before heading up the stairs to go to bed.

The next morning was a Saturday, which was usually the day my sisters and I were allowed to sleep in. However, since we were permitted to spend our money however we pleased, we all opted out of the extra rest in exchange for an early-morning trip to the corner store.

We carefully crossed the busy road between the yellow painted parallel lines and stepped onto the sidewalk. The excitement mounted in my heart. Completely overtaken by anticipation, I skipped joyously past the unoccupied gas pumps in the parking lot. Normally, as the youngest child, I only got to choose from the smallest candies at the store. This usually meant trying and failing to get an adequate sugar rush from a single piece of gum or the smallest of lollipops. But, now, with a whole dollar to spend, for the first time I could choose a large, packaged treat. My salivary glands tightened and drenched my mouth, as I could almost taste the tangy flavors. Choosing between the sweetness of rainbow Skittles and strawberry Starburst, or the delectable taste of sour Mambas, would be virtually impossible because I wanted them all.

The three of us stood in front of the store's entrance before I placed both hands flat on the glass door and lunged forward with all my might. The momentum of the door swinging on its hinges caused the bell tied to the long vertical crossbar to jingle and signal to the clerk that we had arrived. Taking in this moment with all my senses, I noticed the fluorescent lights buzzed slightly and a small radio played muffled tunes in the background. I usually greeted the clerk when we walked in, but today I selfishly decided to put pleasure over my manners.

Leaping between the two aisles housing the bulk of the candy, I glanced wildly from bin to bin. My excitement escalated as I contemplated the huge decision before me. Originally the plan was to buy a large bag of rainbow Skittles, but the euphoria from seeing all the brightly colored, shiny packaged candies caused me to second-guess my decision. Seeing that my budget was one dollar, I decided to make the choice that would bring me the most enjoyment.

Narrowing down my options to just two, I weighed my choices between two fifty-cent candies. Now and Laters gave me a variety of three different flavors: grape, lime, and fruit punch. Each flavor had six one-by-one-inch squares, for a total of eighteen candies. This seemed like the obvious choice because I loved the flavors, however this candy was so hard that you would not have the satisfaction of chewing it. Mambas came with five sets of four different flavors: strawberry, orange, lemon, and raspberry. This option gave me twenty pieces of candy, each chewy and delicious. I was sold. Picking up the Mambas, I walked to the checkout counter.

"Hey, Chaunté, I thought that you were going to get the king-size bag of Skittles," Tania quizzed.

"I was, but I decided to get the fifty-cent candy instead, because I will still have enough left over to also get a Blow Pop and five pieces of gum."

"That's smart! I'm going to do that too, but I'm going to get Now and Laters instead of Mambas."

Wow, Tania called me smart! With a smile on my face, I walk directly up to the cash register to get the lollipop and gum and complete my purchase. Still too focused on the purchase to look up, I rudely ignored pleasantries with the clerk yet again and selected a sour apple Blow Pop and five pieces of Bazooka Bubble Gum. Finally finished with my shopping, I looked up and was startled to see an unfamiliar figure behind the register. It wasn't the normal guy, who stood at average height, with blond hair and blue eyes. Instead, in his place stood a very tall and stately woman with a short Afro and big brown eyes. Like me, she had very rich, deep brown skin. Being in a small town with not many Black families, I thought that I knew all of us, but this was a woman I had never seen before. To be quite honest, I had never seen her or any person who looked like her in my entire life.

She was stunning and I was absolutely captivated as I studied her. She was a stranger to me, and just being in her presence made me a little bit nervous.

Lost in my own thoughts, I realized that not only was I staring at this woman without saying a word, but that she was also glaring back at me with an intense curiosity. Her look caused me to snap out of my internal dialogue and begin to feel afraid. The fiery darts of her gaze sailed past my eyes and pierced my soul. Leaving the candy on the counter, I dropped my arms at my sides and began to walk slowly backward without making my purchase. Mouth agape and heart pounding, I knew I had seen this look on my mother's face before and I also knew that it meant that I was in trouble. Taking one more step backward, I felt a warm body press against my back.

"What are you doing, Chaunté?"

Without turning around, I realized that I had bumped into Tania as she was approaching the counter.

"Little girl, who is your mother?" the woman questioned sternly. More intimidating than this woman's stature was the booming roar of her voice. So smooth and deep, each word she spoke seemed to originate from the depths of her belly. Rich and full of sound, her question once again made my heart pound.

"Little girl! Who is your mother?" she thunderously repeated.

Afraid of getting in trouble for not answering an adult when spoken to, I squeaked out, "Natalie, ma'am."

Wide-eyed and mouth propped open, Tania stood frozen next to me wondering what I had done to get into so much trouble.

Once again opening the glorious instrument that was her mouth, the woman said, "Go home and tell your mother to come up here. RIGHT NOW!" Determined to put more distance between my aggressor and me, I retreated toward the exit door. Tania stepped up and paid for her candy before Alexis did the same. Never taking her eyes off me, the woman rang up each of my sisters' purchases. I could tell she felt justified in exercising her authority over me and this made me feel uneasy.

Leaving the store empty-handed, I walked home in shock. None of us said a word until we knew for sure that she could no longer hear us.

Tania was the first to break the silence.

"What did you do, Chaunté?" she asked.

"I didn't do anything!" I exclaimed as I tried to convince myself that this statement was the absolute truth. I mean, if I really hadn't done anything, how could this woman be so mad at me?

"You didn't even get your candy," Alexis said before dropping her head and moping with me in solidarity.

Looking down at my empty hands, I realized that she was right. My breathing both quickened and shallowed as tears welled up in my eyes and cascaded down my cheeks.

Dropping my hands to my sides, I began to cry inconsolably, when I was interrupted by the softest touch in both of my palms. Closing my fists around something small and warm, I brought my hands up to my eyes to see three Now and Laters in one hand and several Skittles in the other. My team didn't let me down. We earned our treats together and they made sure that we got to enjoy them together. The walk home seemed to go by way too fast, as it always seems to do when you are walking to your own doom. Rather than going straight into the house, I paused for a moment to gobble up my treats. After all, what did I have to lose? I had no idea how much trouble I was in, and who knew when I would be allowed to eat candy again?

The tears were still drying on my cheeks when our door swung open before any of us had even reached for the knob. To my surprise I was met with the comforting face of my maternal grandmother. I jumped into her arms, relieved at the fact that I had an unexpected advocate I knew would take my side and help me get out of trouble.

"Mom, Chaunté's in trouble!" Tania yelled before we set foot inside the house.

"No, I'm not! I didn't do anything," I protested.

Stepping out of the kitchen, my mom looked directly into my eyes and said, "What is this all about, Chaunté?"

"I don't know," I said with a sour whine. "I was at the store buying my candy, and for no reason at all, the lady at the store told me to come home and tell you to come to the store."

"Why does she want me to come up there?" she probed. "What did she look like?"

"I don't know why," I lamented. "She's tall and Black like us and has a really big voice. I think her name was JAN-NEE-TAH." I tried hard to remember the name printed on her name tag.

"Juanita?" my grandmother questioned, chiming in to help us solve this mystery.

"I don't know. Maybe," I said.

"Juanita Booker?" my mom questioned, but this time directed the question toward my grandma instead of me. "Is she back in town? And more importantly, what does she want with me?"

Squinting my eyes and tilting my head to listen more intently, I began to think to myself. *Wait a minute, my mom knows this woman? And if so, how come I've never met her?*

Now sitting on the couch, I looked on with anticipation as my mom and grandma tried to unravel the mystery.

The more they talked, the more I realized that whatever was going on was big and had absolutely nothing to do with me.

Finally, the light bulb went off in my mom's head. I knew this because she gasped before she stood frozen, wide-eyed and staring into nothing like a deer in headlights.

My grandma Beatrice seemed to notice my mom's epiphany at the same time that I did. "What is it, Natalie?"

"Prentice," my mom said. Just one word, nothing more and nothing less.

My grandma gasped and clapped both hands over her mouth.

Now both of them were staring at me and studying my face the same way the stranger did earlier.

I knew Prentice. What did my mom's childhood friend have to do with this? He was nice. I remember being really young and him taking me to the store to buy me a teddy bear, but that's it.

Springing into action, my mom said, "Tania and Alexis, you stay here. Keep the door locked and don't let anyone in. Me, your grandma, and Chaunté are going back to the store."

That's when I realized it wasn't me who was in trouble. It was my mom.

The walk back up the street was full of nervous energy. My mom walked so fast that I had to jog to keep up. Looking to my right, I was surprised to find that Grandma was moving just as fast. Power-walking together, we quickly reached the store and directly approached the register.

"Well, hello, Natalie," said the stranger, who apparently wasn't a stranger at all.

"Hi, Mrs. Booker," my mom sheepishly replied.

Getting straight to the point, Mrs. Booker pointed at me but looked straight at my mom and said, "Who is this girl's father?"

Not giving her a straight answer, my mom only said, "Uh . . ." It was clear that she wasn't trying to be defiant but was truly in shock.

Driving the point further home, the woman pointed at me yet again and said, "I know my family, and that little girl right there is my granddaughter."

Feeling that this woman was deeply mistaken, I waited for my mom to correct her. Then to my shock, my mom said, "Yes, Mrs. Booker, I think she is."

My mind was blown. Wait! What?

How?

Then with the same one word my mom had used earlier, the woman looked at my mom and questioned, "Prentice?"

Once again, my mom sheepishly said, "Yes."

Now the woman looked at me and flashed me the most gorgeous, love-filled smile. Running from behind the counter, she stooped down and gave me the warmest, fullest embrace.

This was nice. She smelled like flowers and the warmth of the sun. Backing up but staying close enough to take me by the hands, she asked me, "What is your name, child?"

Now smiling I said, "Chaunté, ma'am."

"Well, Chaunté, I am your granny! I am so happy to meet you."

Excited and still confused, I smiled wildly from the deepest parts of my heart but chose to not say much.

"You know what?" she continued. "When you left earlier you forgot your candy. Get whatever you want, and I'll pay for it."

I couldn't believe my ears. "Really?!" I exclaimed in disbelief.

"Absolutely," she affirmed before pointing me to the candy bins.

I looked to my mom for approval; she nodded her head yes and sent me on my way.

Diving in, I grabbed a king-size bag of Skittles, a large pack of Now and Laters, Mambas, and three candy bars. Not knowing if I would ever get an opportunity like this again, I also grabbed three sodas and three Blow Pops. Feeling like I might have pushed the limit of this generosity, I timidly dropped all the items on the counter, and she happily rang them up and paid for them.

After exchanging information, she told me that she would be seeing me really soon before we walked out the door. When we got home, my sisters were dumbfounded to see me with so much candy. Remembering their kind gesture of sharing with me earlier, I gave them each a can of soda, a candy bar, and a Blow Pop. After all, we were a team.

Not fully understanding what had just happened, I felt like I had just won the lottery. I'm sure that I had the right to be upset and to ask several more questions about how and why Mrs. Juanita Booker was my grandmother. If I dug a little deeper, I could have focused on the fact that I had just lost the father that I knew and that my sisters were actually my half sisters. But instead, I chose to focus on the facts that I had just gained a grandmother, that I was able to repay my sisters' kindness with a kindness of my own, and that today was the best day of my entire life. I chose love instead of loss and anticipation instead of anger. In time those questions would answer themselves, but for now I was excited about getting to know the amazing woman who had turned my world upside down in the most unexpected way.

3

CLASSROOM CHAMPION

KNOWING THAT I was running out of time, I whooshed and whirled around the house, trying to get ready to go. "Duck, Lex, I'm jumping over you," I said while flying through the air. As this was a routine maneuver, Alexis instinctively tucked in her arms while dipping her head low to make sure I could easily clear her frame.

"You better hurry up because you don't have much time," she said. Landing on the other side of her, fully clear of her body as she sat perched in the bean bag chair, I ran to the end of the hallway before sitting down on the floor to put on my socks and shoes. I grabbed my jacket and wristwatch and studied the bedroom floor to look for my notebook. "Where is it?" I whined in a panic as I began searching among all the toys lying everywhere, my school backpack, and unfolded clothes thrown all over the floor. I couldn't find my notebook anywhere.

Just when I was about to give up, I spotted the pink glitter pad peeking out from underneath my backpack. "Yes, I found it," I exclaimed before picking it up and heading back down the hall toward the front door.

"Oh shoot! I forgot a pen." I pouted and slapped my hand on my forehead. Realizing that the notebook would be useless without something to write with, I headed back down the hall to retrieve one. At 5:00 p.m., to the minute, two quick honks blared from the horn of the yellow Cadillac now waiting outside. "Oh no, she's here." I panicked.

Too excited to keep her waiting, I abandoned my plans to retrieve my pen and headed toward the front door. Knowing how important documenting this trip was to me, my mom stood by the front door, kissed me, and handed me a pen. "How did you know?" I asked, marveling at my mother's intuition. I hugged her and thanked her before heading out the door.

I saw Granny Booker's smile greeting me as I dashed down the sidewalk to the driveway. Cheesing from ear to ear, she motioned for me to hurry up and get into the car. When I met her, she promised that I would be seeing a lot of her, and over the last four years, she'd kept her word. Every chance she got, she took me on a new adventure, exposing me to unique experiences and allowing me to see life through her eyes. Today, we were going to her favorite fishing hole.

Curious about the timing of our trip, I questioned, "Grandma, why are we going to the pond in the evening? Don't most people go fishing before the sun comes up?"

Helping me understand better, she explained, "The fish bite the most just before dusk. So, if we want to catch a lot of fish, this is the best time to go."

Having never been fishing before, I was so excited to see what all the fuss was. However, even more thrilling than this new experience, I was planning on executing a secret plan.

"Hey, Chaunté, what have you got there?" my grandma asked, while peering over her right shoulder at my notebook.

"Well, every time we go out, you tell me the most amazing stories, and this time, I want to write them down. That way, when I go back home and tell my sisters, I won't forget anything."

My grandma, chuckling at my initiative, was very careful not to be critical of my ambition. I think that even at an early age, she saw a lot of herself in me. She'd had experiences that were larger than life, and always encouraged me to dream big and then go after it with everything that I had. "Well, all right, then, what do you wanna know?"

Kind of nervous about being put on the spot, I mustered up enough courage to ask the one question that had been racing through my mind ever since my mom shared the information with me.

"So, my mom told me that you sang for President Reagan's inauguration. Is that true?"

Amused by the serious tone of my question, she let out a deep roar of laughter. "I knew this question was coming, and the answer is yes. I sang our national anthem, 'The Star-Spangled Banner,' for President Reagan's inauguration in January of 1981." Pausing her story, she pointed to my pad and pen and said, "Come on, now, you said that you were going to tell my story. You better do it with excellence and get all the facts correct." Accepting the challenge and feeling up to the task, I fumbled with my pen and pad before listening attentively, carefully taking in every detail.

Writing as quickly as I could, I followed along as she continued, "Most people's dreams start at much younger ages, but mine came true when I was forty-five. I'd fallen in love with singing when I would sing on the farm with my sisters in Arkansas. We grew up in the church, so we would sing the spirituals that we learned there everywhere. It would help the time pass when we would have to work on my daddy's farm.

"Everybody who knew me knew that I loved to sing and would often ask me to sing when they had special events. The event that changed my life was a political fundraiser in 1976 in Paso Robles, when I was asked to sing 'The Battle

Hymn of the Republic.' Just like I always tell you to do, I planned to do it with excellence. My dream was to sing in Carnegie Hall. So, each performance, I would sing like I was singing in Carnegie Hall."

Not wanting to misunderstand a single detail, I interrupted, "What is Carnegie Hall?"

Tickled at being able to share her knowledge with me, she theatrically answered in her most regal accent. "Oh, darling," she said, stretching out the "dar" and over-enunciating the "ling," "it's only the most prestigious concert stage in our entire country."

"Wow!" I marveled before getting the chance to ask my follow-up question. "Did you ever get to sing there?" I said before putting my pen promptly to my pad to record her response.

Not wanting to diminish the quality of her impressive accomplishments, she redirected my question by saying, "Well, eventually I got to sing on a stage that I didn't even dare to dream that I could be on."

"Was that the White House?" I quizzed as I hung on her every word.

"Yes, it was," she responded.

Amazed by the fairy-tale nature of her story, I loved the fact that every word of it was true. "Please tell me more," I urged her, with my pen and pad in hand.

"Treating each stage like it was Carnegie Hall, I sang my heart out at that fundraiser. After I finished, Mr. Ronald Reagan, the California governor at the time, took the stage with tears in his eyes and gave me a huge hug. It was apparent that my song had moved him deeply. He told me that he had heard this song many times before but never heard anyone sing it the way I did. He followed up by proclaiming that if he ever made it to Washington, he wanted me right there by his side singing him into office."

Continuing, she said, "Unfortunately, Mr. Reagan did not win that election. However, like you and me, Mr. Reagan was not a quitter. It took three tries, but on the third try, he won the presidency and was elected to office as the fortieth president of the United States. Holding to his promise to me, he invited me to Washington, D.C., to sing the national anthem at his inauguration."

Gleaming with pride, I said, "I can't believe that someone in my family . . . my grandmother . . . was a famous singer."

Excited and inspired, I dropped my pen and pad down on my lap and just looked at her. I took in every dimple and curve of her face, and for the first time, looking at her, I could see myself.

Peering into her eyes, I imagined seeing what she saw as she stood on that stage in front of thousands of people and sang our nation's most prized song. I understood that she had an amount of bravery that I longed to have in my own life. At that moment, I felt like I too had the right to dream big dreams and possessed everything that I needed within me to accomplish them, which included one day standing on my own stage in front of hundreds of thousands of people as an Olympic athlete.

Once we arrived at the watering hole, we met my grandfather. He was a quiet man who didn't say much, but his presence oozed love and understanding. He owned his own business as a butcher, and everyone knew him for his kindness and generosity. One by one, he took out our poles and lined our hooks with wiggling live nightcrawlers. Casting each line deep into the water, we began to pull out several biting fish. I'd never seen so many fish before, and I couldn't believe that I was catching my own dinner. This day was truly inspirational and one I knew I would cherish for the rest of my life.

When I got home, I gave the fish wrapped in butcher paper to my mom, and she placed them in the freezer. She had already cooked dinner, so I knew we would not be enjoying my catch tonight. Taking a bath and hopping into bed, I got ready for school the next day.

The next day was Friday, which was my favorite day of the week because it was the day we usually had pizza for school lunch. Many kids brought lunch to school, but I always got hot lunch from the school cafeteria because our family took part in the free lunch program. Grabbing the silver rectangular tray holding the pizza wrapped with foil, an apple, and a carton of milk, I headed down the line toward checkout.

Finally, at the front of the line, I was greeted by a friendly cafeteria worker. "Hi, Chaunté, how are you doing today?" she said.

"Hi, ma'am. I'm doing well. Thank you for asking," I responded.

"All right, it's your turn to put in your number," she said.

Stepping up to the numeric keypad, I punched in my number while reciting it under my breath. "Star 9627, enter."

Mouth salivating and tray in hand, I walked over to my usual table and spotted my two lunch buddies, Tiffany Painter and Kayla Weaver. "Hi, guys," I said joyously while sitting down and placing my tray on the table.

"Ooh, what's for lunch today?" Tiffany said as she leaned over to get a better look.

"It's pizza!" I said happily, as I had been waiting for this meal all week. "What about you, Tiff? What do you have?" I said, peering into her purple lunch box.

"The same thing I get every day," she said as she pulled out a turkey sandwich, string cheese, fruit punch Capri Sun, and fruit snacks.

Usually, I was slightly envious of other people's lunches because free lunches did not always have the best options. This envy was especially true on the days where they gave us those runny mashed potatoes with large, chewy chunks of mystery meat and the most disgusting form of gravy. Don't get me wrong, I was happy to get to eat each day, but some meals were easier to swallow than others. Today was one of those days. School pizza was the absolute best.

Even though things were better for our family financially, they were still not great. I was so grateful to have a meal, but punching in my number to get my free lunch was a constant reminder that we couldn't afford several things that other kids could. I was used to getting that feeling from lunch but didn't expect also to get it from the conversation around the table today.

After eating her lunch of sour gummy worms, chips, and soda, Kayla paused in between bites to get the conversation going. "So, has your class gone to the book fair yet?" she asked us both.

Tiffany jumped right in. "Yes, we did! Wasn't it amazing?" she said while wildly flashing us an ecstatic grin.

Kayla continued, "So, what books are you two going to buy from the book fair?"

Tiffany, still excited, could barely contain herself when she blurted out, "I'm going to get the book with the slap bracelets and the one about horses."

Obsessed with puzzles, Kayla said, "I picked the brain teasers and the *Guinness World Records* book."

Satisfied with each other's responses, both of them turned their attention toward me. "What are you going to get, Chaunté?" they asked.

Knowing that this would be a situation in which I yet again would stand out as the one who couldn't afford anything, I looked for any way to wiggle out of this conversation. "I don't know," I said. Trying my best to bluff, I further explained, "Our class hasn't gone to the book fair yet. So, I guess I'll figure it out when I get there."

Always trying my best not to lie, I had indeed told them the truth. Our class had not yet gone to the book fair, but I was sure that I would not be buying a book when we did. I was embarrassed and didn't want to share my poverty woes with my school friends. Without even seeing the prices, I was sure that there would not be a book there that I could afford because I had zero dollars and zero cents.

My lack of money made me quite sad, as I had fallen in love with books when I was able to be part of the summer reading program at our local library. Every year when the Scholastic Book Fair came along, I was excited to see the colorful, shiny covers lining our school library. I had not yet gotten the chance to take home a book of my own, but each year my teacher always bought new titles for students to share within our classroom bookshelves. More books than you could count, accompanied by toys and pictures of adventures, were shipped to our school to be shopped by hundreds of anxiously awaiting boys and girls. Usually, I would look on longingly as the other kids, filled with excitement, surveyed the shelves and picked which books would be going home with them. But this year had to be different. I had to find a way to buy a book of my own.

Rushing to finish my lunch, I scarfed down the last bites of my pizza and hopped merrily outside to the playground. I noticed that the end of recess was approaching, so I lined up against the fence for the last-call race against the boys. Jumping off the start line and sprinting unmercifully across the soccer field, I giggled slightly after beating my classmate Andrew to the finish line for the second time this week. Though our speed was usually evenly matched, besting him today was just the pick-me-up I needed to forget the events of the cafeteria. The whistles blew, signaling to us that it was time to go back to class. Sweaty and slightly exhausted, my sour mood was sweetened by my victory and thoughts of my Olympic future.

All thirty-two of us, still dialed to ten from an energizing lunch and exciting recess, buzzed loudly, with several conversations filling the classroom. Standing in the corner of the room, Mrs. Yarborough, our teacher, flickered the lights off and on three times, signaling that it was time to give her our attention. "One, two, three, all eyes on me," she said before pausing to wait for us to comply. She continued, "As many of you may have heard by now, the Scholastic Book Fair is currently visiting our school. Most of the classes have gone to the fair this week, but our class is scheduled to go next week.

"As a reward for having to wait, I have a special announcement." The roar of excitement once again took center stage and caused us to begin to talk over our teacher. "Hush, students, you will want to hear this," she cautioned before continuing. "Since our class is focusing on a unit in literacy and creative writing, and taking into consideration many of my bright young students are very competitive, I am proposing a contest. This will be a writing contest, and the person who wins will get a certificate for free books from the book fair."

I couldn't believe my ears. This certificate was precisely how I would be able to get my first book from the book fair. I wasn't sure how the other students felt, but for me, the stakes were high. I knew that I had to do everything in my power to make sure that I wrote the best paper to win the prize.

Excited and wanting to make sure that I fully understood the rules, I raised my hand and began wiggling my fingers as high in the air as I could get them. Pointing at me, my teacher said, "Yes, Chaunté, you may speak."

"Mrs. Yarborough," I said. "Does it have to be creative writing? Can I write a nonfiction story?"

Taking a minute to think about my question, she said, "Yes, if you're excited about writing it, I can't wait to read it."

This opportunity couldn't have been set up any better for me. Looking down at my pink glitter notebook, I knew exactly what I was going to write about. Telling my grandmother's story to my entire class would not only give me the opportunity to brag about the woman who shared my family lineage but would also give me a chance to win my coveted prize. I knew it would take work, but I was determined that this book credit would be mine.

Not even waiting for her to finish her sentence, I began to write. Letting our creative minds run wild, she allowed us to take the rest of the day to work on our papers. Having until Monday to finish, I decided not to go outside over the weekend but to work on my masterpiece, only stopping for church on Sunday.

To my surprise, by Monday morning, our classroom had a new seating arrangement when I walked in the door. I didn't like it at all. Mrs. Y had taken all of the chairs and placed them toward the edge of the classroom in a square shape. Each of the desks was facing inward, and now we were all able to look at one another. I was super embarrassed about my clothes, but I was able to hide the dingy spots, the holes, or the tattered and torn garments when I was facing the front of the classroom with nobody looking directly at me. With this new seating arrangement, I felt like a spotlight was shining on me.

Feeling exposed and uncomfortably visible, I worried that everyone would see me for the poor girl I really was. I sat down at my desk and put my backpack on the back of my chair. I crossed my ankles in front of me as I did every day this year, resting on my heels with my toes pointed to the sky. When I looked across the classroom, I saw my classmate James looking at me. Staring at my face and working his way down, he gasped as his gaze reached my feet. I knew immediately that he must have noticed the secret holes on the bottom of my shoes. Trying not to show that I had noticed, I placed my feet squarely on the ground and avoided making eye contact with him for the rest of the day. I sure hoped he didn't tell the other kids what he saw.

Too determined to win to let embarrassment defeat me, when it was my turn, I stood in front of the class and told them the story of my granny. She, the forty-five-year-old mother of six, committed to giving her all to go after her dreams. Not deterred by the challenges that life handed her, she never quit until she sang for the president, by committing to excellence and bravery. Disclosing the biggest secret of all, in the end, I said, "She is my grandma, and my grandma represents the possibilities of what I can achieve when I grow up. She took these giant steps as a pioneer so that I would know that I am capable of significant steps one day too, and so are you!"

Met with claps and a roaring round of applause, I smiled widely before taking a bow. Immediately, hands all across the class were raised high in the air, signaling that my teacher and many of my classmates had questions. They all wanted to know if the story was true.

Impressed, my teacher identified me as one of three finalists. As the votes trickled in from my classmates, I came out on top as the classroom champion and was awarded the ten-dollar certificate to the book fair.

The next day it was our class's turn to go to the book fair. Excited to shop, I settled on the mystery section and grabbed the latest Goosebumps thriller. Holding it in my hands, I felt truly accomplished. To everyone else, it might've looked like I was just holding a book, but to me, I was holding my first competitive medal. Who knew that all competitions didn't happen on the field and that you could actually compete in the classroom with academics?

⌒

As if this week couldn't get any better, Granny Booker paid me a surprise call. "Chaunté, your grandma's on the phone for you," my mom said, before handing me the phone, which dangled from its coiled cord attached to a base on the wall.

"Hi, Grandma. What's going on?" I said, excited to hear her voice.

"Well, hello, little girl. I'm calling to see if you want to go somewhere special with me tonight."

Knowing that every time with Granny was a good time, I said yes before learning what she had in mind.

Honestly, I was looking for a reason to leave home. All the catch from our fishing trip was eaten, and now we would have to make a trip to the community food bank. The whole process was exhausting. I was so grateful to have food, but I was also embarrassed that my friends might see us entering the building. When we went inside, there were a couple of chairs that were super uncomfortable to sit on. There weren't enough for our family of four, and that often meant I would have to sit on the cold, hard floor.

The wait seemed to take forever as my mom shopped the shelves of food that community members had generously donated. As much as I didn't like to be hungry, the food was often old. And many times, we had to eat around mold or stale parts of bread that we were gifted. The food bank was one of my least favorite places. Being able to avoid this trap and spend time with my grandma was something that I knew I wanted to do.

"Where are we going?" I said, anxiously awaiting the details of our latest adventure.

"Well, I want to take you to your cousin Kevin's football game tonight, because it's a very special night for him."

"Wait, I have a cousin Kevin and he plays sports? How cool is that?!" I said, shocked that there were more athletes in my family. Covering the phone receiver, I shouted out as loud as I could, making sure my voice reached every corner of the house. "MOM, CAN I GO WITH GRANNY TO A FOOTBALL GAME?"

Within seconds mom yelled her reply. "SURE, IT'S FINE WITH ME."

Happy to have received permission, I uncovered the receiver and let my granny know I could go. Eager to get ready, I said, "See you soon," before hanging up the phone and rushing through the house to prepare.

Before we even got to the stadium at the high school, I noticed that there were tons of cars parked along every roadside and driveway. We stopped in the park, still a ways off from the football field, and began to walk almost a quarter of a mile to get to the action. Along with us were several other people walking with various items in their hands. Some had bleacher chairs with a back support, others carried flags with team names and colors on them. My grandma pulled out two bleacher chairs, a cup of iced tea, and a cylindrical cone.

When we walked up to the bleachers and looked for a place to sit, I noticed that people began to whisper and stare. I figured everyone must be staring at my grandma because she was famous, but I was mistaken.

What started as whispers grew louder, as those already seated greeted us with cheers. "Yay, she's here," I heard several people say before looking in our direction and giving an excited round of applause.

"Yes! The party can get started now," shouted another fan.

It seemed like they were clapping for my grandmother. I knew that I, personally, thought she was terrific, but I was kind of confused about the relationship these people had with my grandma.

Is this what happens wherever she goes? I wondered silently to myself.

Finally, I heard the announcer say, "All right, football fans. Get ready to welcome your Paso Robles Bearcats."

Taking the field were several young men with burgundy jerseys and shiny, colored helmets. The crowd cheered wildly as they waved back at us and took their positions on the side-line. The other team ran out and did the same, but I noticed that the cheers for them were not as loud. Finally, the players took the field and as they stood in formation, the ball was kicked in the air and the players ran after it. Running one another down and throwing each other to the ground, the fight for victory was underway. After an enormous build of anticipation, our team caught the ball. I was told this was an interception. In a change of directions, the ball was now run toward the field's other goalpost, prompting our side of the stands to cheer wildly.

Grabbing her cone, my grandmother stood up at the front of the stands, turned her back to the field, and faced the crowd. Yelling unprompted and with her mighty voice, she questioned, "What do we want?" in a battle-cry fashion.

The crowd chanted back, "A touchdown!"

She continued, "When do we want it?"

They demanded, "NOW!"

The chanting was repeated continuously.

"What do we want?"

"A touchdown!"

"When do we want it?"

"NOW!"

I was shocked and impressed at her boldness and ability to harness and direct such a large crowd of wildly screaming fans. They weren't excited that she was there because she was famous. They were excited she was there because she was the team's best cheerleader. Following in her footsteps of bravery and boldness, I made sure to stand at her side and join in every time she picked up her megaphone.

At halftime, my grandma leaned over to me, pointed at the field, and said, "This is what I wanted you to see."

Lining up across the field were several of the home team football players. Over the loudspeaker, the announcer said, "All right, sports fans, get ready to honor your seniors." Several of the oldest boys took off their helmets and stood to acknowledge the crowd. Among those boys was my cousin Kevin. One by one, the announcer stated the players' names and their accomplishments up to that point as the crowd cheered and screamed wildly.

When they came to my cousin Kevin, the announcer stated that he would be given special recognition. "For tonight's final senior, we would like to acknowledge Kevin Hill. While we're sad that he is leaving, Kevin has received a full scholarship to play Division One football while attending the University of Idaho, where he will play football and run track."

More thunderous and impressive than the other cheers, the crowd roared with excitement and celebration for my big cousin. I looked over at my grandma as she cheered the loudest. Pride in her eyes beamed as she looked down at me. Wanting to join in on the excitement, but not sure what was going on, I looked at my grandma and said, "What does all this mean?"

Taking this very critical moment to purposefully direct my life, she said, "This means that Kevin is going to change his life forever. He has good grades and is good at sports. So, a university is giving him a scholarship, which means they will pay for him to go to college. Everything he needs will be absolutely free, and when he's done, he is going to be able to get any job that he wants and live the life that he wants." Waiting for my reaction, or just checking to see if I grasped the enormity of this moment, she stooped low and took my hands.

Looking into my eyes she said, "The life that you're living now is not the life you have to have when you grow up. I know that you can change your life by doing what Kevin did and using sports to earn a scholarship, but you must understand that education is the key to shaping a different future for yourself."

I was so inspired. My grandmother never directly addressed our poverty; however, I'm sure she had to have noticed the tattered clothes I sometimes wore and how hungry I always was when she picked me up. I'm also sure the fact didn't escape her that whenever we went places together, I never had money to spend. Instead of merely taking care of my needs only when she saw them, she also offered a solution that would extend well beyond the years during which I was within arm's reach of her care.

I now knew that I could not only compete on the field but also in the classroom. I too could be awarded a scholarship that could change my life. After winning the writing contest and seeing my cousin standing on that field, I knew that my dream had grown. Now, not only was it my goal to be an Olympian, but I was 100 percent dedicated to being a classroom champion as well. I was going to earn a scholarship and go to college. In college, I would be professionally trained for the Olympics. Every step I took from now until then would be to accomplish my dreams of both graduating college and becoming an Olympic athlete. I would change my life forever so that my kids would never have to go to bed with stomach pains from being hungry. The life that I was living now would not be the life I lived when I grew up.

4

PLAYING FROM THE
SIDELINES

BUNDLED IN THREE-STRIPED Adidas jackets, blond, brown, and red bangs blew in the wind as rosy-cheeked faces peered through our third-grade-classroom windows. Chilled fingertips plunged deep into pockets, searching for fleeting slivers of warmth radiating from our bodies as we waited for our teacher to let us inside the classroom. A long monotone beep cascaded through the loudspeakers, piercing all the doorways and halls, prompting each teacher to release the floodgates holding back our school's five hundred eager learners.

Once inside, I hung my backpack on the back of my chair. Getting right to work, I made a beeline for the table of all my athletic friends.

I was on a mission. Determined to make each of my proclamations about myself come true, I decided to find a team by questioning my friends. Having raised the bar on my current life's plan, I decided not to waste a single moment in getting there. Now that I knew that youth sports existed, there was no way that I was turning back to making up workouts as I went along and hoping that I would stumble upon the right training plan. I wanted to find a team that would provide camaraderie, sports education, and structure right now.

Based on the examples around me, I sort of thought that the lifestyle that you were born into was the one that you would have to stay in for the rest of your life. However, my grandmother taught me that this was not true. For the past few years, I dreamed of being an Olympian, running on the world's stage, and achieving my goal, but I never really thought about the life that came along with it. I knew many people who had started college but none who had finished. I saw college as a rite of passage for ambitious people but not a life goal that people completed. After the football game last Friday night, however, that all changed. My cousin was going away to college and would change his life forever, and I had decided that I was going to do the same.

Finding a way onto a sports team was now my new obsession. Before last Friday, I thought that I would have to wait until I was an adult to begin my athletic dreams, but I realized now that if I did enough digging, there was a possibility that I could start realizing my dreams today.

"Hey, Tiana. Did you know that kids can play team sports?" I said, having no clue what her response would be.

"Uh, duh," she quipped sarcastically. Tiana was a classmate with blond hair and rosy cheeks, whose backyard fence was catty-corner to ours. She was a girl who seemed to love sports as much as I did. "Of course I did. We all play soccer on a team together at Sherwood Park."

I couldn't believe my ears. This was a hole in one! In my first time asking, I found my team. That park was only about a five-minute walk from my house. It would be so easy for me to get there. Entirely naïve to the process of getting on a sports team, I jumped right in and began my most sincere plea toward getting an invitation to be a part of their team.

"Well, you already know I love sports, and I'm fast. If I pinky promise to work hard, would you guys let me play on your team?" I said, holding my breath for her reply.

Without even a second's hesitation, she lit up before agreeing to let me on the team. A resounding "Yes" came not only from her but from the other classmates who overheard our conversation.

I was fiercely competitive, and every day that I got the chance to play soccer at recess, I brought intensity and raw talent that usually ended with our team winning. "You're going to have so much fun, but so you know, team soccer is different from recess soccer," Tiana said.

Oh, I thought as I pondered what she'd just said. Learning the game was not an obstacle that I'd considered, but I was sure that I would find a way to adjust to all the differences. All jumping in at once, several of my friends tried to explain team-soccer rules simultaneously. Not being able to zero in on one particular voice, I became slightly overwhelmed at their excitement before the teacher broke up the action to begin class.

Exhilarated and finding it hard to focus, I composed myself, remembering the longer-term goal had two parts and included going to college. Being a winner on the field would come after school, but at this moment, I needed to focus on being a classroom champion.

Paying close attention to my teacher's instructions, I focused intently on her every word. Today, I dedicated myself entirely to mastering each part of her lessons more than any other day before. By the end of the day, I was exhausted, but this was a different type of exhaustion. My brain hurt from all that I had tried to absorb, and my eyes were tired from focusing so intently on the board. Toward the end of the day, I could not wait for the bell to ring, and when it finally did, I packed my bag and headed for the door. I usually skipped out of the classroom hyper and full of energy, but today all I could think about was getting home and taking a nap. Walking down the sidewalk and crossing the street, I remembered that my day was not finished yet. Today was my first day of soccer practice, but I had no idea what time I needed to be at the park.

"Hey, Tiana, what time is the practice today?" I said, yelling back toward the school and across the street.

"Five thirty p.m.," she exclaimed as she climbed into her mother's minivan before sliding the door closed.

Having finished my homework in class today, I decided to jog home rather than walk to have enough time to take a nap before practice. Reaching the front door of the house, I swung my backpack off my left shoulder, slinging it to the floor. Not wanting to waste a single moment, I yelled loud enough to be heard throughout the entire house, "Hey, Mom, I'm home."

"Hey, sweetie," she echoed back from somewhere in the house.

Too tired to walk to her, I yelled again. "I'm going to bed; I have soccer practice in an hour and a half." This statement confused my mom, prompting her to visit my room.

"What do you mean, soccer practice?" she questioned, as this was the first time that she had heard anything about my youth sports ambitions.

"Oh, I joined a soccer team, and they meet at the park at the end of the street at five thirty."

"Oh, okay. Make sure that you are home before the streetlights come on."

The streetlights were our common means of determining time. When they came on, it was time to stop playing and head home for dinner for almost all the kids in the neighborhood. The goal was to get home before the streetlights came on. However, if you were one of the unlucky souls caught out when the lights came on, it was in your best interest that no matter where you were or what you were doing, to drop it and run home as fast as you could.

I was fully aware of the impending punishment awaiting me if I broke the streetlight rules. I confirmed and complied by saying, "I know, Mom. I will be back home in time." Drifting off to sleep, I slept an hour and a half before it was time to go.

When I woke up, my stomach ached with the familiar pains of hunger. Even though I knew it was unlikely that there was something in the refrigerator, I still walked over to the cooled white box and opened the door. Peering inside, I saw ketchup, mustard, and a bag with two bread ends crumbled within it. I knew that I could settle for my usual ketchup sandwich, but today I just wasn't in the mood. Trying my hardest to ignore the growls and whispers of my quaking, empty belly, I decided it was best not to even think about food and just head to practice with an empty stomach. It wasn't that big of a deal. By now, I was used to it and knew that I could eat breakfast tomorrow at school.

Not knowing what to wear, I put on a pair of shorts, a T-shirt, and a pullover hoodie before dashing out the door. I was too excited to walk, so for the second time today I took a brisk jog. When I reached the park, I could see that the other kids were already there, stretching and counting in unison as they stood in a circle on the field. Just like I had seen at the football game last week, each player wore a matching jersey with a number on it.

Taking a place next to Tiana, I jumped right in and began stretching. Being the only African American person on the field, I must have stuck out like a sore thumb because the coach noticed me and pulled me out of the circle before I could even finish my first ten-count. Looking around at the spectating parents, the absence of any African American mothers probably made it evident to this man that I was there alone without a supporting cast.

"Hey, you in the purple hoodie, come with me," he said with a stern hand placed firmly on my back. My heart was thrown into a state of confusion, as suddenly its intense beating caused by excitement turned to unexpected fear. Walking me outside the earshot of the other kids, he said, "Who are you?"

"My name is Chaunté," I said with a slight quaver in my voice.

"This is a closed practice, only for kids on our team," he barked at me.

Relieved, I exhaled deeply, able to breathe a little easier. Now smiling, I answered, "Oh, that's not a problem, I am on the team. My friends from school said it was okay for me to be on their team."

Tilting his head sideways and shifting the weight to the back of his neck, he squinted his eyes and flashed me a confused stare. Opening his mouth to reprimand me further, he said, "Well, they can't do that, because this is my team."

Hearing those words caused my breath to quicken, and a wave of heat overwhelmed my chest. "If you want to be on my team, you need your parents' permission and to pay the fee."

Grasping for any bit of hope as my sports dreams began to slip through my fingers, I blurted out, "Oh, wait, I do have permission; my mom said that I could play." Looking into his eyes, I hoped that having one of his two requirements would be enough for him to let me play, at least for today. In my mind, I thought that maybe if he saw me play and just gave me a chance, he would see value in my potential and we could work out the payment stuff later. His matter-of-fact stance and his crossed arms gave me more insight into his thoughts than his eyes ever could.

Looking at me without blinking, he said, "You can't play because you still have to pay." Staring me up and down, he paused to look at my ratty hoodie before stopping to gaze at my Kmart-brand shoes, and said, "It's more money than you have."

Not wanting to give up, I continued to attempt to negotiate the terms of me being part of the team. Out of desperation, I said, "How much does it cost?"

I knew I didn't have money, but maybe if I knew how high the bar was set, I could come up with a way to earn it. After all, this was a kids' team, so the cost would have to be in reach for kids to be able to pay for it.

Absent of emotion, he responded without an ounce of inflection in his voice. "It's $175 for the season," he said. "Plus the cost of the uniform, and you have to be able to afford our tournament to China later in the year."

Upon hearing this, my heart sank to the dew-drenched grass. I thought the cost could have been $10 or maybe $20 at the most. If that was the case, I had already begun devising a plan to collect cans for the remainder of the year and exchange them at the recycling center to cover the fee. That plan would have taken a lot of work, but I was willing to do whatever was needed to be on that team.

The burning in my chest intensified as I realized that $175 was way too far out of reach. Even as a child, I would instinctually count all the money coming in and out of the house. My mom made $535 per month to take care of herself and us three girls. The state aided her with $120 in food stamps with the sole purpose of buying us groceries. In addition to those resources, the only other source of income we received was from my sisters' father, which was $50 per month in child support. In total, we only had $705 per month to cover $800 per month in household expenses. Having done the math long ago, I knew even as a child this was not enough to make ends meet. Somehow my mom made it work, but I knew it was not easy. There was no way that I would dare add the burden of my goals to her plate, so I concluded in my heart that I would not even ask.

There was nothing more that I could say. I knew that paying for soccer was out of the question. Standing there staring at him in disbelief, internally I crumpled to the ground and curled into a ball from the pain of dashed hopes. Outwardly, however, I just looked at him, hoping he would change his mind about me and have mercy. With no such luck, he looked at me and, with a final act of brutality, used a dismissive hand gesture to wave me off the field. Choosing to add insult to injury, he turned his back to me, leaving me to feel shunned and ashamed. Frozen where I stood, I was unable to move. "All right, you have to go now. This is a closed practice and is only for paying players."

⌒

Unable to hold in my emotions any longer, I cried uncontrollably as I exited the field with my head down. Not looking back to see if my friends saw what happened, I left, embarrassed and defeated. Helpless and hopeless, I swung on the swings watching from a distance as they practiced. Not wanting to return home and answer questions about why I had come back so early, I sat on a swing trying to make sense of what had just happened. As my sobs softened and tears dried, my sadness began to churn into a fuming tornado of emotion.

Talking to myself, I lamented, "Who does he think that he is? He doesn't own the park. This is a public park, and he can't say who can be here and who can't." Looking over at the team, I realized that from this vantage point, I could see them, but they couldn't see me.

Still fuming, I began a game of, "He can't stop me from . . ." and stating ways I could toe the line to exercise my rights to be at the park and what he couldn't stop me from doing while I was there.

It started with, "He can't stop me from being at the park."

Then progressed into, "He can't stop me from watching."

Which grew into, "He can't stop me from learning."

Until I finally settled on, "He can't stop me from practicing over here by myself." I accepted the fact that I could not be on the team, but I refused to deny myself the opportunity to learn from experienced trainers. Hiding within the cover of the trees, I pushed my weight forward and powered off the swing. Standing alone, I began to do drills with the team. I copied my friends as they learned from their coach on the field with high knees, karaokes, and wind sprints. As they ran from cone to cone, I ran from tree to tree. Empowered and free, I pushed myself to execute each drill as though I was being meticulously watched and corrected.

Once practice was over, I jogged out of the park and ran home. Upon entering the house, my mom asked how soccer practice was. Smiling at her, I said, "It was great," without mentioning a word about what had actually happened.

As far as I could tell, until I graduated college, I knew money would always be a barrier to my goals and aspirations. I didn't particularly appreciate living like this. Instead of allowing this barrier to be something that stopped me right in my tracks, I made a pact with myself that every barrier I faced would be perceived as a personal challenge. I began to expect and welcome these challenges because I knew that I became stronger and wiser every time I could find a way around them. I had to allow this moment to remind me to keep fighting even when the work got hard.

Every step I took toward my goals was a step away from a life of poverty. I would have to be patient and persevere, but I knew that I would eventually get there if I didn't quit. The stakes were too high, and I believed in the end result. So, each Monday at 5:30 p.m., in the shadows of the trees, alone, yet together with the team, I trained not for what I could get from it today but for what I would be destined for tomorrow.

5

STATE TRACK MEET

THROUGH THE SQUARE-SHAPED glass, I realized we were surrounded by farmland for as far as the eye could see. I let the car window down and stuck my arm outside. Tilting my hand up vertically to feel the velocity of the wind pushing against it, I allowed myself to melt into the relaxation created by nature's massage. Bending my hand back and parting my fingers, I let the cool breezes peeking through the hot air squeeze between my digits. You would hardly believe that we were barreling down the highway at seventy miles an hour because I felt so peaceful and calm.

This trip was now the third time I took the 160-mile trek from Paso Robles to San Jose, California, for the track-and-field Hershey Regional state championships. Three years after the soccer field fiasco, I had now found my place on a recreation track team. We were the Paso Robles Cheetahs. Fast and fierce, our caravan of cars cascaded down one of

California's most famous highways, the 101, carrying our team of eager athletes to the regional championships for the third time. Having aged out of the track team, my sister Alexis did not join us this time.

Over the past three years, I had come to believe that everything worked itself out with time. A couple of months after being barred from the soccer team, Alexis and I received a flyer from our school.

"Chaunté, did you read it?" Alexis teased in excitement. "Did you *read it*, read it?" she pressed.

"No," I finally admitted. "What's the big deal anyway? It looks like a coupon for Taco Bell. What use is that to me? To use a coupon, you still have to have money to pay for whatever you are getting at a discount."

Beginning to feel frustrated with my dismissiveness, she shoved the paper in my face and sternly said, "Read it." Finally yielding to my sister's persistence, I peeled the paper away from my eyes, and began to read:

> Taco Bell track meet. The winner of each race will be awarded a free taco redeemable at your Taco Bell located at 1107 24th Street. Tryouts for the team relays will be at lunch tomorrow. Participation is entirely free.

I couldn't believe what I had just read. Making that team was one of the happiest days of my life. Unbeknownst to us, that meet would serve as a tryout to represent our town's team at the California Hershey Regional State Championships in June. Having had the joy of devouring several free tacos, I was now on my way to competing in my third state championship meet. Coach Henry Jenkins had a vision for this team. He was a genuine man with a heart of gold, and putting this team together was his pride and joy. He didn't charge us to participate. We only had to get to practice, buy a generic uniform made up of the team colors, and find a way to get to the state meet.

Even though we were riding down the same road I had traveled two times before, everything in my life looked different. The first time we took this trip up north, my mom, Alexis, and Tania were with me. My mom's mother, Grandma Bea, drove us, and we had the most fantastic time. Nestled tightly in the back of her golden Dodge Omni, we three sisters rested our heads on one another's shoulders and nestled into each other in the close space. Sharing stories of race strategies, we planned how we could win our races and help our team. To expend nervous energy, we played "slug bug" and playfully punched one another in the arm every time we saw a Beetle car throughout our nearly four-hour drive. While competing was the objective of these trips, the memories of our time together left deeply cherished imprints on our hearts and minds for a lifetime.

I thought that it would always be like that, but this time was different. In the fall a couple of years ago, chill breezes weren't the only phenomena filling the air between us and the endless sea of cirrus clouds. Somehow in the expanse of patterned blue and white waves rippling the sky, my mom, shot by cupid's arrow, found love.

Melvin was a handsome man with a solid athletic build and an Afro that would provoke many men to envy. His days as a college football player in Ohio were still evident by the toned cuts lining the muscles of his rippled arms and legs. He made my mom happy, so naturally, we were over-joyed when they were married.

All the happiness of new love faded when he began to drink heavily and started beating her. The last time he used her as his punching bag was so brutal that he left her bleeding with a fractured skull and spiraling into a deep depression.

No matter how hard I tried, I couldn't get that night out of my head—awoken in the middle of the night to bang-ing on the walls. I ran out of my room to see my mother hunched over the brick fireplace and holding the back of her neck. My stepdad, irate, stood over her with a broken glass bottle in his hand. Her sobs were faint whispers as she seemed to go in and out of consciousness. Becoming aware that we girls were awake and out of bed, she seemed to take comfort in knowing that we were there to halt the frequency of the blows. I knew she needed help, but how could I protect her from him?

After looking to my sisters, we simultaneously unleashed the loudest, most blood-curdling screams that we could to sound the alarm and end his attack. It was working. The louder we screamed, the farther he backed away from my mom. That was good, but it wasn't enough.

Still powerless against this athletic man's brute strength, we strategized to defend our mom against our stepdad. The only possible weapon we had to fight him with was finding a way to bring the police to our house to arrest him.

Looking to the wall where our phone once hung, my heart sank when I realized the service had been suspended for nonpayment.

"Chaunté, you're the fastest, you have to run and call 911," Tania said, commissioning me to leave the house alone in the middle of the night. "Run, Chaunté, go get help!" The entire time Tania gave me directions, Alexis never once stopped screaming. We knew it was the one thing saving my mom, and she was not willing to stop, even for one second.

I ran out of the house as fast as I could as my chest burned against the damp night's air. I knocked on the door of a neighbor's house, and a disheveled man opened it. Seeing a look of distress on my face, he leaned in close to hear what I was going to say.

"Excuse me, sir. My stepdad's hitting my mom, and she needs help. Can I please use your phone to call the police?"

With a look of sorrow in his eyes, he said, "Sorry, I can't help you," and closed the door in my face. I didn't have time to be offended. I just left and looked for another way to accomplish the mission.

I knew that any payphone would allow me to call 911 free of charge, but the nearest payphone was half a mile away. It didn't matter. My mom needed my help, and I had been training my entire life for this moment.

I ran down the street that usually crawled with kids, pets, and people occupying the sidewalks. It was empty, lonely, dark, and scary this time, but I didn't care. I ran against the dark of night as fast as I could, ignoring the pain in my legs and chest.

I still can't believe the police came so quickly. Watching my stepdad being carried away in handcuffs hurt. I loved him. When he wasn't drunk, he was an amazing father, but he was a monster under the influence of alcohol. Although our family was now broken, at least we girls were still together.

This trip to the track meet would be a much-needed break from the harsh reality waiting for me at home.

My stepfather's arrest and removal from our home didn't stop my mom from missing extensive work, which caused her to lose her job. Understandably, the lack of income made the financial situation at home more difficult.

In a desperate sign of surrender, my mother asked Granny Booker to take me in for the summer to make it easier to take care of my other two sisters. I was okay with this plan. I saw it as a great adventure and a way to hear more of those fantastic stories that my granny shared with me. Burying my feelings about our home turmoil deep down inside, I welcomed the distraction that track season would bring. Out on the track, I didn't have to talk or feel. All I had to do was run. So, each day, checking my feelings and problems at the gate, I ran my heart out, ignoring my present circumstances and looking ahead to my future goals.

This time, in year three, I took the trek solo to San Jose, riding with my coach and his family instead of my own. My maternal grandma, Bea, had relocated to Southern California, and my sisters had aged out of the program, leaving me to compete on my own. All season I had been planning to compete in the 100-meter race and the relay; however, an unexpected event caused all of that to change.

"Hey, Chaunté," Coach Jenkins said when I got into the car. "There has been a change of plans, and your team needs you." Not having the thrill of being needed since the day of dishwashing for allowance many years ago, I was all ears, eager to answer the call. "Jessica Blum was supposed to run the 400 and the 800, but her grandfather passed unexpectedly. Can you fill in for her in the 400?"

Not even taking time to digest the implication of what he was saying, I replied, "If the team needs me, I will do it." Many experienced track runners would attest that there is a monstrous difference between running 100 meters, which is one-fourth of a lap, and running 400 meters, which is one time all around the track.

The whole point of practicing was to prepare our bodies to handle the race that we were best suited for. That was the plan, but now all of that was out the window. I would be running my race and one of hers.

Finishing my shorter race, I now prepared for the 400-meter. Looking at all the other girls who were also preparing for this race, I decided to copy their prerace strategy. If they high-kneed, I high-kneed. If they did a wind sprint, I did a wind sprint. I didn't know what to do or how to attack this race, but I figured that my best shot at doing well was to copy those who did.

The wait for the 400-meter races was finally over. As we lined up in heats of eight, I watched three heats go ahead of me before I would begin running in heat four. Up to this point, I carried unearned confidence that quickly imploded when the reality of my fate began to kick in. In race one, I saw the girls line up staggered on the curve of the track. The starter said, "Runners, to your marks." This prompted the girls to step up to the line. As the second command, he said, "Set." Each girl crouched down, getting ready to run. Then he blew a whistle, signaling that the runners could go. To my shock, when the whistle blew, the runners did not shoot out like a cannon. Instead, they galloped out, controlled and relaxed. However, even though they weren't going fast, I noticed that toward the last straightaway of the race, the kids began to slow down dramatically and would have to fight to get to the finish line. After crossing the line, most of the kids collapsed and fell to the ground, and several of the kids began to cry and gasp for air.

One race after another, I saw this same pattern repeatedly. Eyes wide from sheer shock and terror, I looked around at my coach. Before I could run to him, he ran to me. "What have I gotten myself into?" I said. "I can't do this. Please don't make me run."

Placing his hands on both sides of my head, he looked at me and said, "Just go out there and do your best. That's all we're asking. If you do that, you'll make us proud." At the time, I didn't know what it was, but his words of positive affirmation fueled me deeper than I had ever been fueled before.

Choosing to face the fear head-on, I took the last few moments to strategize a plan based on the races that had gone before me. What I'd learned was that no matter how the runners started out, they all seemed to lose all steam during the last 100 meters of the race. My race strategy was simple. I would push out at the start with all my might and run as fast as I could for the first 300 meters. Then when everyone hit the point where they get tired, I would be so far ahead that no one would be able to catch me.

Each of the runners was staggered in their own lane; the starter said, "Runners, to your marks." Stepping up and placing my toe just behind the line, I looked forward, very pleased with my clever plan. "Get set." Crouching forward in the ready position, I listened intently for the first sound of the whistle. *TWEET!* The whistle blew, and unlike all the other girls, I flew out like a cannon. Plowing my way down the track, I was aware of the gasps and cheers of the spectators in the stands and those lining the fence. Using my peripheral vision to survey the right and left of me, I was pleased that there was not a single runner anywhere near me. Coming to the 200-meter mark, I was still alone. I couldn't believe that my plan worked. I was going to win this race.

Just when I felt like I would safely secure the win, something unexpected happened. I felt my shoulders slump and I became aware that I had less control of my arms. I could no longer bring my arms all the way up to my face, as they now seemed content to swing low and stay down at my sides. In further defiance, they also began to protest, going back and forth, and instead swung wildly from side to side.

Without any notice, my legs began to follow suit. I simultaneously felt a burn radiating from my hamstrings to my gluteus, and a numbness dulled the feeling in my quads. Using my thoughts, I told my legs to get it together and to execute the running form that we had practiced. However, they just ignored me and decided to go rogue. Realizing that I was still 100 meters from the spot where I was supposed to get tired, I knew that I was in trouble.

Choosing to be more stubborn than the body that was giving up on me, I yelled at my limbs, "Come ON." Determined not to let the others catch up, I battled with my body in a tug-of-war for submission for the next 80 meters. Refusing to yield, I finally won the battle by the time I reached the 300-meter mark. Now in control of my limbs, I could see the finish line. Defiant and scared of losing, I did what I had not seen done before. Instead of succumbing to unwelcome deceleration, I fought it and ran with all my might to the finish line.

Crossing the finish line first, I couldn't believe that I had controlled that race from beginning to end. That was literally the hardest thing that I had ever done in my entire life. The thrill of the win was powerful but not powerful enough to overcome the tragic end awaiting any person who decided to run a 400-meter race all-out with no training. Gasping for air, the lactic acid building up in my hamstrings shot pain from the soles of my feet to the middle of my back. I was trying to crumple to the ground, when I was carried off the track and redirected to the grass infield to recover.

Finally, lying on the grass, I panted, desperate for the pain to end. Suddenly, in the steaming, 100-degree weather, I got goose bumps all over my body. Just as quickly as my body chilled, my mouth began to water, and my stomach turned sour. Noticing my distress, one of the track officials brought a trash can over and picked me up just in time for me to deposit everything I had eaten in the last twenty-four hours.

This experience was completely new to me. I had never felt like this after the 100-meter run. Even though running all-out made me physically sick, for some strange reason, I felt an immense amount of pride and accomplishment for fighting my toughest battle and winning.

I flew high with endorphins all the way home. I couldn't believe the warrior that I had become. All I could think about the entire ride home was telling my mom and sisters about the epic battle that I was just in and how I came out victorious.

When we finally got back to Paso, I walked into the house and asked Granny Booker if she would take me home for the weekend. I loved being at her house but wanted to share this joy with the ones who had been on this ride with me ever since I watched my first Olympics at four years old.

Waiting for her response, I could tell that something was off. Looking at me with sadness, she said, "Chaunté, we need to talk."

Quiet and scared, I said, "Wait, let me feed Ziggy first." Ziggy was my pet rat. He was the only pet that I ever had that was all my own. I asked my grandmother to pet-sit over the two days that I would be out of town and wanted to see him before I was given any bad news.

Looking at me sadly, she said, "That's the problem; Ziggy has died." I was so upset with her. I was only gone two days. How could she let him die like that? Livid, I once again buried my emotions and called my mom to come take me home.

Packing my bags, I waited for my mom and said goodbye to my grandma. Surprised to see my mom in the car without my sisters, I jumped in and rode all the way home without talking about my loss. Choosing instead to focus on the victory I'd had at the meet, I told her about my epic battle on the track and the fact that I threw up after my race. Not as talkative as usual, she smiled occasionally and nodded to show me that she was listening. When we got home, I was confused to see tons of furniture on the lawn.

Hmm, I thought to myself. "Mom, are we having a yard sale, or are you cleaning?" Sometimes when my mom shampooed the carpet, she would take all the furniture out of the house and put it outside. Leaving my belongings in the car, I ran into the house.

Yelling loudly for my team, I stood in the doorway and waited for my sisters to descend from various parts of the house. Puzzled that they didn't come running, I ran to our bedroom. Alexis wasn't there. I ran to Tania's room, and she wasn't there either. By process of elimination, I knew that they would be outside. Zipping past my mom to get to the sliding glass door, I was stopped by my mom grabbing my arm. Trying to break free of her grip, I pulled away from her, now panicked that I couldn't find my sisters.

"Chauntè, stop," she yelled. "They are not here. They don't live here anymore. They got on a train this morning and moved away to live with their dad." I couldn't believe my ears. She had to be lying. My mom would never send my sisters away, especially to go live with their dad. He was an absent father and had not taken an interest in them their entire lives.

Distraught, I screamed at her, "How could you do that? You didn't even give me a chance to say goodbye!" I was angry. I was hurt, and I was scared. My entire world had crumbled, and I had been left alone in the ashes and rubble. Refusing to express my emotion, I became numb. I didn't cry, and I stopped arguing. Not talking to her or even looking her in the eye, I began to look around the room. I had been so focused on finding my sisters that I hadn't noticed that the whole house was completely empty. Staring at the door, I saw what looked like an official document with a bright red stamp on it. Walking closer to get a better look, I stood in front of the door and read the letter to see what was written on it.

Three words inked with that stamp explained the entire situation. It read, NOTICE OF EVICTION. Gasping, I understood what had happened. We were being thrown out on the street. Rather than let her daughters be homeless with her, my mother had placed each of her babies on a life raft while choosing to go down with the sinking ship alone. Looking back at her, I ran to her and put my arms around her as she sat on the floor with her face buried in her hands. Sobbing loudly and painfully, her tears streamed from her eyes, and I held her until she fell asleep. Keeping watch over our belongings, I let her rest without disturbing her for several hours. Once she woke, she took over the shift of watching our things, as we were expecting the sheriff to put us out in the morning.

I went to the bathroom to shower and wash my face. Looking in the mirror, I realized that for the first time in my life, I was going to need to put my dreams on hold and be there for my mom in any way that I could. At that moment, my goals did not matter. If my mom chose to go down with the sinking ship, I would be there right by her side. There was no way I was going to allow my mom to face this trial alone.

As expected, the sheriff knocked on the door at 6:00 a.m. Since there was nothing in the house to gather, we just left. Searching the boxes outside on the front lawn, my mom refused to give up until she found what she was looking for.

"Ma'am, you need to leave this property," the sheriff said while ushering us away from the house that we still knew as home.

"Okay, I'm going. Just give me a second to find something," she said, defiant and strong.

Still feverishly looking, she finally located three specially packed boxes and smiled as she loaded them into the car.

I was wondering what was so important that she risked getting in trouble with the law to save. I jumped into the back seat and opened the boxes. My heart melted as I saw every doll that my sisters and I had ever owned, every report card and principal's honor roll certificate that I had ever earned, and every ribbon that I had won from all the Taco

Bell track meets that I had ever competed in. Even amid her turmoil, she held on to everything that was important to me. Her love for her kids superseded any personal tragedy that she now faced.

Throwing a child out on the street like this shouldn't be legal, yet it was. And a sheriff-escorted eviction was forcing us to go. With a million thoughts swirling in my head, I only dared to scream within my mind, *How is this even fair?* My mom was the victim of domestic violence, healing from the damage of a fractured skull. Yet we were the ones who were now homeless. As we drove down the street, I looked out the car window and watched my friends play as though nothing in their world had changed. But as I looked back toward my lawn at all my belongings, I realized my entire life was being left behind, and there was nothing I could do about it. As I thought about this fact, each breath seemed harder to take in. I felt a burning sensation when I inhaled, as though prickly air was filling my lungs.

All my hurt welled up inside of me like an over-inflated balloon about to burst into a million pieces. *I have to relieve this pressure somehow*, I thought to myself as dizziness began to blur my vision from the back of my eyes.

Exhaling seemed virtually impossible as my heart began to beat thunderously within my chest. The sensation of needing to weep washed over my entire body, overwhelming me with sadness. It became clear that the only way to make this burning stop would be to cry, but I refused. Not wanting my mom to see my pain, I began to mentally plug each open hole of my broken heart with the hopes I clung to for my future. I began to envision each dream I had dreamed about my life as a student-athlete coming true. The more I focused on it, the better I felt.

I knew I would eventually have to let the pent-up emotions out, but for now, in front of my mom, I would allow the joy and hope for my future to overwhelm the pain of my present. To my relief, it worked.

For the first time, I didn't see my mom as my mom, but as a woman who was strong, amazingly fierce, and resilient. No longer crying, she looked in the rearview mirror, wiped her face, and said, "All right, Chaunté, come up here to the front seat and buckle up. We need to find a place to live." Putting the car in reverse, we drove away from everything comfortable, secure, and familiar, leaving the life we had built together on the lawn. As we drove, I was so happy that my mom did not have to do this alone. Choosing not to look back, we drove forward into the unknown, determined that whatever challenges we faced, we would face them together.

6

HOMELESS SUMMER

TOSSING AND TURNING from one side to the other, I realized that I was not going to get any more sleep. Grateful not to be sleeping outside, I wouldn't dare to complain about not having a mattress to lie on. As my mom slept next to me, I glanced at the gold watch on her wrist and realized that it was time to get up anyway. Rubbing my fingers against the smoothness of my pillow, I searched for a prickly spike from a vein of a feather. Once I felt one, I tugged at its stem and held the feather between my thumb and index finger. I crawled on my elbows combat-style and slid my body closer to my mom and leaned over her face. Taking the feather, I tickled her nose and then laid down quickly to pretend that I was still asleep.

As I watched her swipe at the tickle on her nose, I buried my face into the carpeted floor and giggled at my silly prank. Choosing not to mess with her anymore, I kissed her on the forehead before saying, "It's time to get up, sleepyhead." She rolled over toward me, grabbed the back of my neck, and pulled me in for a hug.

"Good morning, sweetheart," she said.

"Good morning, Mom," I said back.

I was finally used to this new routine. I bent down to pick up my makeshift bed, made from blankets and sleeping bags. I folded them up as neatly and compactly as possible and set them near the door. Walking to my backpack, I pulled out my clean outfit, toothbrush, and towel, and headed for the bathroom. After exchanging my outfit from the day before, I put on my clean clothes before brushing my teeth and washing my face. Looking in the mirror, I was so happy that my mom had cornrowed my hair. Even though I was homeless, I didn't want to look like it. These thin rows of neatly woven braids clung close to my scalp and gave me the freedom to not have to fight with my tangles every day. This elegant, low-fuss hairstyle made it easy to get up and out of our host's home in a short amount of time.

Each day of this summer had been generally the same. After sleeping on the floor in the home of a friend or an acquaintance, we would rise early in the morning, pack our things, and head out to face the day. Before leaving, I took a second look to ensure that I didn't leave anything behind before turning off the light and heading to the kitchen.

I believed I overheard someone call our host from last night Teresa. She was an acquaintance of my mom's, but someone I did not know at all. Always wanting to be a grateful guest, I made sure to express my gratitude to each of our hosts. "Ma'am," I said, truly uncertain of her name. "It was nice meeting you. Thank you so much for letting us sleep here last night," I said before making my way to the front door.

"Oh, honey, you're more than welcome to stay here whenever you need," she said as she looked around her kitchen. Walking to the cupboard, she began to pull items out and asked, "Would you like to take some food with you?" She began putting fruit and snacks into a shopping bag.

Looking to my mom, I interpreted her glaring at me to be a sign of disapproval before I politely declined. "No, thank you. Letting us stay here was more than enough."

My mother, being a very independent woman, frequently refused help, even when she needed it. She believed that you should only take from others in life-or-death situations, and if you could find a way to make it work yourself, you should. Putting a roof over our heads at night was her highest priority right now, and she didn't want to wear out our welcome by also eating our hosts' food. So, each day they offered, we declined.

Buckling up in the car, my mom put the gear into reverse and headed out to face the day.

"Chaunté, are you hungry?" she said, now permitting me to share my true feelings.

"Yes, Mom. I'm starving."

Taking a detour from our planned route, we pulled into the gas station convenience store. Mom bought me a sixty-nine-cent bean-and-cheese burrito and some Strawberry Quik. After the clerk rang me up, I took the burrito to the store-owned microwave and heated it. It's funny. I had never noticed before, but after becoming homeless, I'd realized almost all gas stations had a place for people to warm up food.

With the sound of the beep, I took my burrito and ventilated one end of the plastic wrapper. It was still too hot to eat and my mouth watered as I waited for my food to cool. Licking my lips, I noticed that they were dry and cracking from dehydration. I walked back up to the clerk and engaged her in conversation.

"How much would it cost for a cup of ice water?"

Looking to a pricing sheet stashed below the register, she said, "Twenty-five cents."

Plunging my hand into my pocket, I pulled out a dime and a nickel before reaching into the shared change dish on the counter and retrieving the other ten cents needed to complete the purchase. The clerk took the money and rang me up without saying a word. I could tell that she was taking pity on me, but I pretended not to notice.

Just as I was about to leave, she built the courage to speak up.

"Hey, your name's Chaunté, right?" she said, trying her best to make me feel comfortable.

"Yeah, how do you know that?" I asked, curious as to where this conversation was going.

"Well, I've known your family for a long time and I wanted to know if you could do me a favor later today," she said in a gentle and caring tone. "During my noon break, it's hard for me to get away from my post to go buy lunch. If you come up here and walk to Pizza Express to pick up my lunch, I will buy you lunch, too," she explained.

The pizza restaurant was only four doors down in the same plaza, so I decided I would take the job without saying a word to my mom. It had been so long since I'd had pizza, and I didn't see it as charity if I worked for it. "Okay, ma'am, I'll be back here at noon."

Walking out of the store, I buckled myself into the passenger seat of my mom's car, and we headed to the park to make a plan for the day. These trips to the park were much different from those we used to take, when I was obsessed with my Olympic training. As I sat on the bench eating my breakfast of strawberry milk and tortilla-wrapped beans, my mom thoroughly examined the newspaper's classified ads, looking for work.

Impressed with how delicious this cheap burrito was, I took breaks from my eating to get the details on our daily plan. "So, how does it look today?" I said, examining the burrito, deciding where to bite next.

Taking a red pen, she circled two jobs before stopping to answer my question. "Well, there's a couple for me to check on today, but we'll see." My heart broke as I noticed the fatigue in her eyes, and I began to look for ways to make the situation better.

Devouring the last bite of my budget breakfast, I crumpled the plastic wrapper in my hands and said emphatically, "I'm here, Mom. What can I do to help?" Fully expecting her to shrug off my gesture, I was surprised when she put down the newspaper and gave me her full attention.

"If you want to help, I need you to pray, because I believe that God has a special ear for the prayers of children." To me, this was not an outlandish request, but I wondered why she picked today to make it.

"Mom, why do you want me to pray?" I questioned, wanting to know as many details of my assignment as possible.

"Whenever you're desperate, you have to remember that the Bible tells us not to be anxious about anything, but in everything make our requests known to God." Looking at her in awe, I realized that she had not let go of her faith through all of this hardship. Choosing to take this moment to learn resilience, I silently listened as she continued. "Besides, we've been at this for two months. Maybe God can do what I can't." Knowing that she was right and that we had nothing to lose, I gave her my word that I would give it my best shot.

After breakfast, we were once again on the move. Driving a mile down the road, we stopped by my mom's younger sister's house. I liked coming here because I got to play with my four cousins. My aunt's one-story greenhouse was always cool, like an oasis in the middle of a summer desert. Furnished with every luxury I wished we had, I loved plunging in their pool after watching Dish TV and finishing the day with tons of fresh fruit, hot barbecue, and Capri Suns.

Not knowing if I would be able to stay, I tuned in to my mom's conversation with her sister.

"Hey, Debbie, can Chaunté stay here while I go look for work?" she asked, even though I know it pained her to do so.

Without hesitation, my aunt Debbie said, "Sure," before opening the screen door to let us in.

As soon as I stepped in, I was greeted warmly by all four of my aunt and uncle's daughters as they each chatted wildly, telling me all their latest news.

I loved my cousins. There was one of them to match each of the ages of my sisters and me, as well as a bonus baby whom we all adored. We'd grown up together and gone to school together. They were the closest thing I had to sisters now that mine were gone.

Once my mom left, my aunt took my bag and washed my clothes as I played with my cousins. Swimming in their pool was always tons of fun, allowing me to get lost in being a kid again and almost losing track of time.

"Hosanna, what time is it?" I asked my eldest cousin as she sunbathed next to the pool, preserving her newest hairstyle.

"It's 11:35," she said. "Why? Do you have somewhere to be?"

"Oh no! Actually, I do!" I said before jumping out of the pool and getting dressed. "Please tell your mom I went to the store, and I'll be right back." By the time I was dressed and heading out the door, it was 11:45, and I knew there was no way I would make it on time on foot. Luckily, chained to the awning in front of their house was a brand-new ten-speed bike that Granny Booker had gifted me. I kept it there because I knew it would be safe while my mother and I lived nomadic lives.

Barreling down the sidewalk, I rode as fast as I could, reaching the storefront at precisely noon. Stepping inside, the clerk greeted me with a warm smile before asking me to buy her two slices of pizza and a fountain cup of Coca-Cola.

Handing me five dollars, she looked at me and said, "Take the rest of this and spend it on yourself." The cost of her meal was three dollars, leaving me two dollars to spend on myself. After ordering her meal, I ordered myself a slice of pizza, a can of soda, and a twenty-five-cent Blow Pop. Content that I had spent every cent of the money I earned, I gave her the lunch I'd promised and rode my bike to the park.

Sitting at the same bench my mother and I had sat at earlier this morning, I opened my lunch and began eating alone. Contemplating her request, I looked around at all the other kids and couldn't help but feel like I was forced to grow up way too fast.

Why is it that some people get to live so good, while others have to suffer so badly? I thought to myself. I had hoped that things would be getting better by now, but every day, no matter how hard we worked, our situation was unchanged by night.

Talking to no one in particular, I noted, "Food sure tastes a lot better when you appreciate being blessed with an unexpected meal."

No longer interested in people-watching or being left alone with my thoughts, I finished up my lunch and headed back to my aunt's house to wait for my mom with our next move.

When I reached the front door, I was greeted by my aunt looking down the street, probably awaiting my arrival.

"Hey, Chaunté, you were gone a long time. I was just about to come looking for you."

Not giving her all the details of my trip, I said, "I'm sorry, I went to the store to run an errand for the lady who works there." Tired, I looked at my aunt with sleepy eyes and asked if it would be okay if I took a nap in my cousin's bed. It had been so long since I'd slept in a bed, and I knew for sure that I would not be sleeping in one tonight.

I could tell her heart broke when I asked this, and she immediately took me to my cousin's room and allowed me to get some rest. Tucking me in tightly and closing the door, I melted in the comfort of cushions and springs. I'd never really appreciated my bed when I had one of my own, but I was grateful for this one now. Not wanting this moment to end, I looked to the door to make sure no one was coming before getting out of the bed and walking to my cousin's closet.

Kneeling, I clasped my hands and began to pray.

"Dear God, this is me, Chaunté. Please forgive me for any sins that I have done and help me forgive people who have mistreated me. I need your help right now. Mom and I are living on the street. We are drained and usually hungry. Can you please make way for my mom to get a job so that we could have a home? Thank you for providing a roof for us every night. I ask these things in Jesus's name. Amen."

The prayer was simple, and I was unsure if I did it right, but I hoped that God would hear me and help us even if I did it wrong.

I climbed back into the bed, where I slept deeper than I had all summer. Feeling a tickle on my nose, I wiped my face before realizing what was going on. As I opened only my right eye, I was not surprised to see my mom's silhouette in the dark room.

"How long was I asleep?" I said, slightly disoriented from unbelievable rest.

"I'm unsure, but we need to go quickly," she said, now searching the room and gathering my things.

"Where are we going?" I asked, slightly concerned with her urgency.

"I found a place for us to stay and a job!" she said, unable to contain her excitement.

Her genuine smile and laughter were a welcome sight after months of grave disappointment.

We had to hurry because the landlord was going to meet us at the property to give us the key.

Now smiling in disbelief, I hopped out of bed and began looking for my shoes. Trying to rush but not forgetting my manners, I found my aunt cleaning up the kitchen and thanked her before walking out the door.

Driving clear across town, I enthusiastically asked my mom for the details of this new job and shelter. "So, tell me everything, Mom. What happened?" She was barely able to get her words out through the width of her smile as she began to tell me about her day.

"After I left you, I went to check on the two jobs and completed both applications. Their process is going to take a little longer than we would like, and I will have to wait to hear back from them. After that, I heard about a double-wide trailer available and went to talk to the landlord to see how much he wanted to rent it for.

"Looking at the space, I noticed that it needed a lot of work and would not be a place that we could live in for the long term. The landlord said if I was willing to do the reno-vations, he would allow us to stay free while the work was being done."

"Wait, for free?" I said, shocked that this opportunity was even an option.

"Yes, completely free. We just have to do the work," Mom said as we pulled into a trailer park driveway.

In front of a sizable baby-blue trailer, awaiting us was an older gentleman with a key in his hand. After signing a contract and taking the key, Mom and I crossed the threshold and entered our new home.

Looking within its four walls, I could tell the mobile home had everything we would need to live: a kitchen, a bathroom, two bedrooms, and a living room. The first room was large. Nothing was in the room, but I was sure that we would figure out furniture over time. Walking past the bathroom, I found my room. To my surprise, in the corner of the room was a mattress on the floor. Complete with pink sheets, a pillow, and a blanket. I knew this bed was mine.

It could have been a coincidence that the day I prayed for help, our entire situation changed, but then again, maybe it wasn't. Either way, that day I gained a more profound belief in the power of prayer and would remember to turn to it at the first sign of distress in the future. Our summer of homelessness was finally over, and for the first time in the last several months, that night I was going to get to sleep in my own bed. Turning out the light, I curled into the darkness of night, and for the first time in a long time, I allowed myself to dream of a life where I would get to be a kid again.

7

SIXTH GRADE

AFTER A TUMULTUOUS summer, a week of peaceful rest in our new home was exactly what my mind and body needed. I had been so preoccupied with surviving that I'd forgotten all about the massive milestone on the horizon.

Looking down at the printed schedule in my hand, I read the first line silently to myself. *Homeroom?* I questioned. *What is homeroom?* I wondered as I looked across the courtyard filled with hundreds of neatly dressed students. I couldn't believe that today would be my first day of middle school. I'd seen both Tania and Alexis make this same leap a couple of years earlier and was excited that it was finally my turn to go through this rite of passage.

They'd always raved about the pizza and freedom you got when you went to middle school—unlike the mass-produced cafeteria pizza of elementary school, in middle school we got pizza from a local restaurant. Round Table catered at our school every Friday, and to me, that day couldn't come soon enough.

Looking down once again at my schedule, I felt overwhelmed thinking about finding all seven of my classes. Usually, you'd learn your schedule during orientation, but I missed the one scheduled for this school because I'd just moved here. Diligently searching the faces in front of me, I sighed in relief when I recognized a familiar face across the quad.

"Oh good, it's Christina," I exclaimed to myself before running to catch up with her. Christina was a family friend I'd known my whole life. Our mothers were friends and had grown up together, reaching as far back as elementary school. Seeing that she was a grade ahead of me, I knew she would more than likely be able to help me and show me where to go.

Stopping in front of her, I screeched with the fear of being late. "Chris, I need your help. I don't know where my first class is."

Taking my schedule and examining the classroom number, she smiled before telling me, "Oh, your class is right next to mine. Just follow me." Relieved that I had found somebody who knew her way around the school, I followed her. Just as she'd promised, I found the trailer with a class number placard that matched the one on my schedule.

I had gone into the day without expectations, but I was surprised to see that we did not have assigned seats. Since I was almost late to class, the only seats available were right in front of the teacher's desk. This was already a vast improvement from elementary school. The freedom of being able to pick your own seat was so empowering. I didn't mind sitting at the front of the class because I'd discovered long ago that it was the best place to learn with the fewest distractions.

Staying true to my commitment to being a diligent student, I took out a sheet of paper and a pencil and placed them on my desk. A couple of the other students snickered and laughed. "What is she doing?" I heard a voice say from behind me, followed by another laugh.

"You don't take notes in homeroom. Doesn't she know that?" said another student. Now, feeling awkward, I looked around the room and realized nobody else was taking notes.

Still undeterred by my commitment to learning, I waited patiently through roll call and announcements for the teacher to begin her instruction. While the teacher was still at her desk, a bell rang over the loudspeaker, sending a loud *BINNNG* through the air.

To my surprise, all the students stood up, began to collect their backpacks, and headed out the door. "All right, students, see you tomorrow," the teacher said, confirming that we had indeed been dismissed. Confused by what was happening, I turned to the student to my left to get clarity.

"Excuse me, can you tell me where everyone's going?" I asked, completely lost in the commotion.

"Yeah, they're going to their next class," replied the girl as she too headed toward the door.

"Class can't be over," I said to myself. "That was only seven minutes."

Overhearing my line of questioning, the teacher took pity on me and gave me the explanation that I was seeking. "Homeroom is only for announcements and attendance. First period will be your first normal class," she explained while ushering me out the door.

Embarrassed, I exited the class with my head down, looking at the schedule now in my hands, hoping that the day would go better than it started.

Luckily it did. The rest of the day went much smoother and came to an end quickly. My last class was language arts and was situated on the second floor of our school's main building.

Looking out the window, I recognized the football stadium to be the same one Granny Booker had brought me to many years before for my cousin's football game. Remembering Kevin standing there on the field as he was acknowledged for earning his college scholarship reminded me that part of achieving my dreams depended on what I did in class every day.

"All right, Chaunté, we know that you can win on the field, but it's time to get your head back in the game and execute your plan to be a classroom champion," I said, encouraging myself in a much-needed pep talk. For the rest of the class, I gave my studies everything that I had, feeling the pride of once again being on track for my goals.

After the dismissal bell rang, I caught up with Christina, who was waiting for me at the school's front. I loved many things about our new home, but one of the best perks was that I was now neighbors with one of my best friends. Enjoying every moment of this unique experience, I walked along the road with the caravan of energized preteens, all still buzzing from the excitement of the first day of school. Trying to decide which conversation I was going to join, I grimaced and shifted my backpack so that the straps would stop digging into the tops of my shoulders.

"What's wrong?" Christina asked, taking note of my discomfort.

"These books are heavy," I said, trying my best not to sound like I was complaining.

"Yeah, seven classes mean seven books. Don't worry; you'll get used to it. Besides, you don't have to do this every day because we get to leave this set of books at home, and we will use the class set when we are at school."

"Thank goodness!" I exclaimed in relief. "I couldn't imagine doing this every day," I said while looking down at the sidewalk, attempting to use my head to counterbalance the weight. Studying the sidewalk, I realized that this path was familiar to me. Reading the cracks and scars of the pavement, I gasped in excitement.

"Are you okay?" Christina asked, thinking something was wrong. "Yeah, I'm okay. I just realized that this is the same sidewalk I used to walk on when I was a kid," I replied.

Remembering the days when I would carry groceries from the store along this same path with my mom and sisters made me sad. Realizing how much things had changed over these years caused me to drift to the back of the pack. I sulked, longing sincerely for the days when we could be a family again, and felt lonely even though other people surrounded me.

What had started as a massive group began to shrink as kids broke off when we passed their homes. Most of the kids walking were my direct neighbors and used the same route home that I did. I was caught off guard when a relatively large chunk of the group, including Christina, veered right, turning off the main road simultaneously.

"Where are you going, Chris?" I said, knowing that this way was a massive detour from our quickest path home.

"We're all going to the rec center," she said, motioning for me to follow.

"What's the rec center?" I said, terrified of getting in trouble for not sticking to the route my mom expected me to be on.

"It's an awesome place we all hang out at after school. They have video games, snacks, and a place to do homework. Everyone's going. Are you coming?"

I stood there for a moment to assess the situation. Looking at the group of roughly fifty kids, I noticed that they seemed to be good, responsible kids. No one was blatantly causing trouble or breaking the rules. I was hesitant because I didn't want to get in trouble, but more important, I wanted to be safe. Making a split decision, I decided to go and veered right with the herd.

Slightly nervous, I turned to Chris and said, "Okay, I'll only stay for a few minutes, just to check it out, and then I'm going home." Now, not as talkative as before, I looked around nervously, taking in every detail of my surroundings with my feet, ready to run at the slightest indication of danger.

Only two blocks off the main road, I saw a basketball hoop and playground enclosed within a chain-link fence. Situated on the far side of the fence was a massive triple-wide trailer, much like those used at school.

Plopped in the middle of our small town's low-income housing projects was what looked like a kids' oasis. Bypassing the gates, we all walked up a long ramp leading to the entrance of the structure. Lining up against the building's wall, single-file, we each waited for our turn to be checked in.

Trying my best to peek in from outside, I was bumped on my left shoulder.

"Excuse us, we need to get past you," I heard a voice say before three girls cut in front of me from behind. Bypassing the line altogether, the girls seemed to know where they were going and were obviously in a rush to get there.

Once I finally got to the front of the line, I saw a girl who had to be only nine or ten years old acting as a bouncer, checking students into the center. With fluffy bangs and sandy brown hair, she extended an open hand toward my direction and said, "Twenty-five cents, please."

Not expecting to have to pay for entry, I plunged my hand into my pocket, hoping that I had some change left over from the school snack. Tucked in its deepest corner, I felt a single large coin and pulled it out of my pocket, revealing that it was indeed a quarter. Relieved to have avoided embarrassment for the second time today, I handed the quarter to the young worker.

"Thank you. Now give me your hand," she said while grabbing my arm. Pulling it close to her, she turned to her side, grabbed a stamp, and pressed the stamp to the back of my hand. No longer blocking the entrance, she stepped aside, giving me access to the center.

Not wanting to explore the center alone, I waited just inside the door for Christina. "How is it that this little kid sounds like a mini adult?" I asked once she stepped in to join me.

Now, seizing the moment to take in the atmosphere, I realized this center was electric. The cool breeze of the air conditioner swirled refreshingly across my face as the buttery smell of fresh popcorn filled my nostrils. Pings, rings, and bells of various video games sang songs of victory for the huddles of boys gaming in the corner. Paper airplanes whizzed in the air as the banging and clacking of a foosball table simultaneously sent two kids into sighs and cheers. *Ohs* and *aws* hummed against vibrating walls of a floor with boys break-dancing. The mood was complete with the rhythmic booms bouncing on the stereo system to the beat of our favorite songs. This place was thrilling.

Taking off my now unbearably heavy backpack and stacking it on top of the mountain with all the others, I looked around to see who was in charge. There was not an adult in sight. Even though everyone was having a good time, this place was so well run that I knew some grown-up had to be in charge. The phone on the wall rang, causing me to immediately turn my eyes in its direction to see the adult who would answer the phone. To my surprise, it was the girl who had passed me up in line who answered the call.

"Oak Park Recreation Center, how may I help you?" she said in the most professional voice I had ever heard a child talk in. "Absolutely, I'll have them ready when you come," she said before hanging up. Stepping away from the phone, she grabbed a megaphone, stood on a table, and said, "All junior leaders, I need you up at the front. Vicky will be here any minute." Suddenly, students from all over the center emerged, wearing red shirts with a name tag and the words *Junior Leader* printed on them. That's when it occurred to me that the kids were running the center.

After assembling, the whole group walked outside to wait in the parking lot, and I followed them.

"Hey, who's Vicky?" I asked one of the junior leaders.

"She's the boss," he answered without taking his eyes off the parking lot. Within minutes, a white fifteen-passenger van pulled into the parking lot and a woman got out very quickly. Without saying a word, she walked to the back of the van, opened both doors, and pulled out a box.

"All right, guys, come on, I can't do this by myself."

Rushing out all at once, the leaders went to the back of the van and began pulling out boxes. I wasn't doing anything else, so I decided to help. Peeking into the box in my hands, I realized it was filled with food: fresh fruit, packaged snacks, and drinks.

"Come on, guys, pick up the pace. They'll be here any minute," Vicky said, already on her second trip to the van. Once the van was fully unloaded, I followed the leaders to the back of the center, over to a table where we stacked all the food. Without being prompted, each leader washed their hands and began to put on gloves. Soon, the front doorway of the rec center was once again filled with lines of people. This time the line was comprised of little kids, babies, adults, and everything in between. As they came in through the front door, each person was led to the back table and then out the back door. People from throughout the entire community were fed within the four walls of that rec center. The junior leaders acting in various positions were running this recreation center and serving their community.

Wondering if this was a common occurrence, I whispered to the leader closest to me, "Do they do this every day?" I was truly in awe of the generosity I had just witnessed.

"Yes, every single day, Monday through Friday." Nobody was charged. They were just given food to eat. Everyone was welcome, with no questions asked. This was a group that I wanted to be a part of. Once all the food was distributed, I ran home to check in with my mom.

"Hey, Mom, I am so sorry that I'm late," I said as I walked in the door. Throwing my backpack in my room, I came back out to see if I could leave again.

"Where were you?" she reprimanded. "You are thirty minutes late."

"I'm so sorry, Mom. All of my friends went to the rec center, and I went with them. They are waiting for me. Would it be okay if I went back?"

Knowing that she would ask a million questions, making it harder for me to leave, I decided to answer all her questions before she asked them.

"Yes, they have a place for us to do homework there, and it only costs a quarter each day. No, I won't talk to strangers or get in the car with any, and yes, I will be home before the streetlights come on. Also, I'll be with Christina, so if it gets dark, we'll walk home together."

Surprised and chuckling to herself, she said, "Well, I guess you covered it all; there is nothing left for me to ask."

"So, can I go?" I pleaded, hoping that she would say yes.

"Sure you can. Have fun and stay safe," she said before walking me back out the door.

On the way back to the center, I decided that I wanted to be a junior leader. Wasting no time at all, I tracked Vicky down and cornered her into a conversation. It was hard to keep her in one place at one time because she was always on the move. "Hi, Vicky, my name is Chaunté, and I would like to be a junior leader." She gave me a good once-over, starting at my head and working down to the once-again-tattered shoes on my feet. Bracing myself for the embarrassment and disappointment I had felt on the soccer field, I expected to hear a rejection.

"Come with me," she said, "and grab a couple of those boxes." She did the same and walked back out to her van. Loading the boxes into the back of the van, she continued. "We have requirements and standards for our junior leaders. You must have good grades, attend the training, cannot get in trouble with the law, and must always be on time. Do any of those requirements exclude you?"

Thrilled that I was being judged by my character and not by what I was wearing, I asserted, "No, I meet all of these requirements."

Taking me on my word, she nodded her head yes in approval. "Okay, your first task is to fill out an application. It's an essential skill that you will use several times in your life. I want it completed in pen. Go slow and take your time.

Fill out all the information you know, and if you don't know the answer, leave it blank, and I will help you. I will not accept any mistakes or scratch-outs on the paper. If you make a mistake, you will have to take another form and start over. You will not use Wite-Out. Do you understand?" she said, looking intently for a reply,

"Yes, ma'am, I do."

"Our junior leaders are just that. They are leaders. This is not a paid job, but one that earns you community service, which is very important for college applications. If you take your junior leadership position seriously and do a good job, there will be a paying job opportunity for you in the summer. How does that sound?" she said, pausing to gauge my understanding.

"That sounds great!" I said, unable to contain my excitement.

Continuing, she said, "Your community service hours here will earn you trips and expose you to many things that you may not be used to. Each day you work, you will log your hours, and the amount you work will either qualify you or disqualify you for a trip. It's on you. Nobody is going to dictate your hours. Each quarter, you need to bring in your grades to ensure that you are still eligible to be a junior leader. And that's pretty much it," she said before asking, "Do you have any questions?"

"Yes, I have one. When can I start?" I said, knowing that there wasn't anything that could keep this job from being mine.

The following week of training was intense. Sitting across the table from other junior leader prospects, we broke up in pairs and practiced the tasks we would be expected to perform during our service. Picking up a toy phone to role-play, I held it to my ear before saying, "Hello, this is the Oak Park Recreation Center, this is Chaunté speaking, how may I help you?"

I looked to my partner for the evaluation, and she giggled before saying, "You almost got it, but you added too many extra words. Try it again." Going back and forth, we quizzed each other meticulously until we got it right. Mastering each skill, from running the concession and keeping a time card to coordinating events, we held each other to the highest standard of excellence that our predecessors had set before us.

My time management skills became well developed. Every day of my sixth-grade year was impeccably planned. I'd wake up early, walk to school, push myself to excel in class, and then head to work at the recreation center. While I ran the streets, my mom worked dutifully renovating our mobile home to keep a roof over our heads.

Finally getting the chance to travel, I earned trips to go skiing, see Janet Jackson perform live, scream my head off at Six Flags Magic Mountain, and attend a performance of *Beauty and the Beast*. I was living the best days of my life. I'd traveled everywhere within the state of California and was rarely home. I was fully committed. And nothing could stop me from earning one of the paid summer jobs.

8

SUMMER JOB

TODAY WAS THE day! I had worked all year long, earning community service hours to prove to Vicky that I was responsible enough to be awarded one of the highly coveted summer jobs that paid a salary. Waking up early and tiptoeing around the house, I got dressed and ready to go without making a sound. It was Saturday, and I didn't want to wake my mom. She had been working hard all year to renovate our mobile home, meeting her end of the bargain to keep a roof over our heads. Looking around at the newly installed cabinets, new flooring, and repaired walls, I was impressed by how much my mom had accomplished.

Heading out the door, I'd realized that I had been so busy working at the rec center this year that I hadn't spent much time with my mom. I felt terrible about it, but my mom encouraged me to go because she knew I was getting exposure to life lessons and experiences that she couldn't provide for me. Many days before walking out the door, I would stop and offer to stay home with her, but she always declined.

Today I didn't look back but wished that I did. If I had known that my time living with my mom was coming to an end, I would have never left.

After a brisk walk to the rec center, I stood in line to look at the paper mounted to the wall. My heart raced to see if I had served enough hours to earn one of the coveted paying summer jobs. Reflecting on the last school year, I couldn't believe how mature I had become—reconciling in my mind that no matter what the list said, I was happy with myself and proud of how responsible I had become.

Stepping up to the paper taped to the brown wood paneling, I gasped in excitement. "I did it," I yelped to myself before jumping in the air. Halfway down the page, highlighted by bolded letters, was my name, indicating that I had reached the milestone. It was official. I would be one of the junior leaders representing Oak Park Rec at the Mid-State Fair. At twelve years old, with a work permit in tow, I would become a wage-earning, tax-paying citizen.

The weeks leading up to the first day of work were filled with intense job training and flew by at a record pace. The dozens of us who were chosen to work drilled one another as we learned the obligations of our new job. When the day finally arrived, I could not have been more excited.

Since my shift started in the late afternoon, there was no need to sneak out quietly as my mom slept. To my delight, my mom wanted to see me off to my first day of work. Instead of letting me walk like I usually did, she offered to give me a ride.

After she dropped me off at the rec center, all those scheduled to work today piled into two vans. The Mid-State Fairgrounds was only a few miles away, so the ride was short. Descending from the van, we all buzzed with anticipation of what our first day of work would be like. The effort it took to get to that moment was hard, but I was so glad that this time had finally come.

With no time to waste, we entered the park and were led to our assigned water stations. The job was fun and straightforward. We'd sit at a shaded cart and sell water to fairgoers. Since we had a short period before the gates would open, I decided to get myself fired up. Looking down at my uniform, I admired the rich blue fabric accented with bright white letters. "Okay, girl! Look at you, looking all grown and stuff!" I said to myself before looking to make sure no one else was around. The cursive word written across my chest read *Culligan*, the water company we worked for. After straightening my name tag, I looked at my cart to ensure it complied with Vicky's customer-service-rules checklist.

The Mid-State Fair was a massive event in our county. People came from all over to enjoy headlining performers like MC Hammer, Kenny G, Garth Brooks, and many more. From July to August, the hot summer sun was brutal and dehydrating. That's where our services came in. We were there to sell parched families ice-cold water. Sitting on my stool behind the cash register, I surveyed my workstation for debris, trash, or other elements that would make my cart uninviting.

Walking to the front of the cart, I took my towel and wiped water droplets from the surface of the countertop. Hearing footsteps behind me, I put away my rag and hurried to get behind my register.

Now able to see who was approaching, I sat attentively to wait for the woman to stand beneath the shade of my umbrella. Looking at the pricing display, she surveyed all our items while she decided what to purchase.

Mustering my most professional voice, which I'd perfected while answering phones at the rec center, I said, "Hello, miss. How can I help you today?"

Taking hold of a fan and two of our largest bottles of water, she said, "This will be all for me."

Looking to the keys on my register, I tapped the button for each item before punching the button labeled *Enter*. Looking at her with a smile, I said, "That will be sixteen dollars and fifty cents." Surprised at the cost myself, I grimaced, waiting for her to scold me for charging her so much. To my surprise, she smiled back at me, handed me a twenty-dollar bill, and waited for her change. Taking the twenty-dollar bill and placing it underneath the cash register, I retrieved her change and counted it back to her.

"Sixteen-fifty, seventeen, eighteen, nineteen, and twenty," I said with accuracy and precision. Once I was able to see that she was happy with the transaction, I placed the twenty-dollar bill in the register and dutifully waited for my next customer.

Proud of myself for successfully making my first sale, I took advantage of the slow traffic to take in the sights. The smell of popcorn, cotton candy, and what I could only imagine were deep-fried funnel cakes filled the air. Warm breezes intensified the one-hundred-degree heat with each gust, causing me to dip my hand in the ice basin right in front of me. Watching people burn from the sun's rays, I was so glad that I had the protection of an umbrella. An alarm bell began to scream defiantly, piercing the air and settling in each fairgoer's ears. A roar of emphatic cheers diverted my attention toward the Strong Man Challenge. A tanned man rippling with muscles flexed for the crowd, screaming in triumph, and the carnival worker handed him a large plush teddy bear.

The entire day went on like this. Families from all around came to the fair to enjoy rides, play games, and connect with old friends. Concert music from over a tall fence filled the air as performer after performer took the stage. There wasn't much time for me to get bored because the heat beating down on us all ensured that I would have an endless supply of customers.

The crowds came one after another, barely giving me time to relax or breathe. Looking down at my cart, I panicked because I'd realized my inventory was nearly depleted, and so was my stockpile of boxes holding the extra bottles of water. I reached toward my left hip and grabbed the black walkie-talkie I'd been issued and mashed the transmitter button.

"Vicky, this is Chaunté at cart three; come in," I said. Another customer came to my stand as I anxiously awaited her response.

"Hello, dear, can I please have a large bottle of water?" she said while handing me the exact change to make the purchase. I tried to hide the panic on my face as I reached deep into my almost melted ice and gave her my last large bottle of water. Taking her money, I placed it into the register when I heard the crackle of my walkie-talkie. "Ten-four. This is Vicky. What do you need, Chaunté?"

Relieved, I held the walkie up to my face to explain my dilemma. "I am almost completely out of water and ice," I said, concerned that she wouldn't be able to get to me in time.

"I figured as much," she said before her end of the walkie went cold.

Confused, it took me a second to process that I had heard her voice in stereo. A response had blared from the device in my hands but also from behind my right shoulder. Turning around, I jumped out of my stool with joy to see Vicky driving up to my station on a golf cart. After helping her unload roughly twenty cases of water and several five-pound bags of ice, I reloaded my cart and was ready for business.

Looking at Vicky, I was impressed with her intuition. "How did you know I was almost out of water?"

"It's hot out here today, and almost all of our carts have been selling out," she said while hopping back onto the golf cart to refill the next station.

"I can't thank you enough for this job. It means so much to me."

She smiled broadly, and I could tell this gave her heart great joy. She said, "I know. You're welcome," and drove off, leaving me to my work.

9

GOODBYE, MOMMY

BEFORE THE NIGHT was done, I had completely sold out of all my water again.

I was stiff and tired from a long day of work when Vicky picked up all of us junior leaders and loaded us into the white rec center van. The ten-minute ride home was quiet. Most of us napped, counting the seconds until we would be able to lie in our beds. When we arrived in the parking lot of the rec, several parents were already there, awaiting the return of their children.

My mom sat there in her brown Dodge Aspen. Usually, I would jog to greet her, but tonight I was just too tired. Sauntering up to the car, I opened the door and plopped all my body weight into the comfort of the passenger seat.

Looking at my mom, I noticed she had prominent bags under her red eyes. "Hey, Mom. It's past midnight. Did you stay up to wait for me?" I said with a look of concern on my face.

Turning toward me as she put the car in reverse, she reluctantly responded by answering my question indirectly. "Well, I've been up this entire time."

I knew my mom well enough to know that there was a reason she avoided giving my question a direct answer. Too scared to get bad news, I decided not to ask any more questions for the rest of the ride home. My mom parked in the spot assigned to our trailer, and I stepped out of the car and walked to my front door. Whatever was going on with my mom would have to wait until morning. All I could think about now was getting into my bed. Taking my key out of my pocket, I unlocked the door and walked inside. However, I wasn't given the luxury of waiting until morning: The answer to what was wrong with my mom smacked me right in the face.

Every visible corner of the house had moving boxes packed with all our home's belongings. My mom didn't need to say a word. My heart sank as I realized that we were being evicted from our home again. Completely blindsided by this news, I looked at my mom and asked a straightforward question. "What happened?" Now I understood why her eyes were red and puffy from tears.

She explained, "The renovation is done, and now the owner wants the property back to sell it."

"Can he do that?" I exclaimed, feeling that we'd experienced an injustice.

"Yes, he can. It's his property, and he can do what he wants with it," she said, fully accepting our new situation.

"Well, can we buy it? I have a job now," I reasoned.

"I appreciate the gesture, but it costs more than we can afford," Mom said with her head hung low.

"So, what is going to happen to us now?" I questioned, yielding to our new fate.

"Well, we must leave by tomorrow, and I'm going to be on the street again," she said, trying her best to hold it together in front of me.

Offended, I retorted, "What do you mean, *you*? We're going to be homeless together." Looking at her face, I could tell that she was unmoved by my proclamation. "Besides, I have a job, and I can help with expenses," I pleaded, fearful that she was going to send me away like my sisters. Unlike my sisters, I didn't have a dad who I could be sent away to. My dad was in prison and had never taken an active role in my life. I didn't like the idea of placing that burden on my granny because she had already done so much for me. I felt stuck in an impossible situation.

Searching for answers with an endless stream of "what if" questions, I hushed long enough for my mom to answer them. "It hurt me to see you homeless with me last time, and I won't let that happen again. You are going to stay with my sister until I can get back on my feet."

Maybe I should have protested more, but I was already so tired from a long day of work. I went to my room and spent the rest of the night packing until the sun came up, and I finally dozed off to sleep.

Around noon, my mother woke me with a soft touch to my left shoulder. "It's time, sleepyhead."

Emotional yet compliant, I got up and grabbed the duffel bags lining my wall and walked out to the living room. "Hi, Auntie," I said, hugging my mom's sister around her neck.

"Hi, lady. Are you ready to go?" she said, trying to rush me toward the door. Looking around, I could tell that my mom had done a lot of work while I was sleeping. The mobile home was now empty, and I supposed the only thing left for us was to go. Hugging my mom, I walked to the door, where the landlord greeted me. Trying his hardest to avoid eye contact, he glanced over my shoulder while asking if my mom was around. Pointing him inside, I stepped around him and headed for my aunt's van.

I couldn't believe this was happening a second time. Once again, my childhood was packed up in a couple of bags, leaving me powerless against the fate that lay before me. My lungs and heart ached as my emotions began to grow dull, and my body felt numb. Staring down the spiraling stairs of despair, I felt as though my foot was about to slip into a deep depression, when I remembered the tactic I had used last time we were evicted.

I began mentally painting a picture of my future far away from where I was now and squarely planted where I wanted to go. Grasping on to every hope of college, I visualized making the Olympic team and standing on a podium.

Putting one foot in front of the other, I once again took the scary steps into uncertainty. That day I vowed to myself that no matter what, I would keep my feet planted on this path, and one day I would have the power to make sure I would never be forced out of a home again.

Once inside the van, I closed the door and looked back toward our home. Without an ounce of defiance, I saw my mom hand the manager the keys, walk out the front door with her two bags, and head to her car without looking back. I could see she was in pain, and for the first time, I knew she had given up her will to fight. To me, it was apparent that she had decided that she was going to go out into the world and let the chips fall where they may.

~

The rest of the summer passed by at a dizzying speed. I worked almost every day that I could while being careful not to spend a cent more of my earnings than I had to. As for my mom, letting the chips fall where they may led her to the mountains of Utah. She paired up with another drifter, with intentions of exploring other states from campsite to campsite. I was happy that she was not alone.

She made sure to call me from a payphone at least once a week, but soon her calls became less and less frequent. Even though I was with family, I felt alone. I can't explain why I felt this way, but I did. Being in a house full of girls who loved me and an aunt and uncle who cared for my needs should have been comforting, but too many of the people I loved were missing. My sisters were gone, and I missed them terribly, and now my mom was gone too.

Getting dressed, I put on my uniform one last time. Today was the last day of my summer job, and I had no idea what I would be doing after. The last day of the fair was a blur. I had gotten so good at doing the same thing over and over that I was now able to do it on autopilot. That night, after my shift, I turned in my name tag before thanking Vicky for providing me with the opportunity to work.

That evening, as I lay on my pillow, I reached into the black sock where I hid my money and counted it—$1,600. I couldn't believe that I had made so much money. Satisfied with all my hard work, I closed my eyes and drifted off to sleep.

The following day, I woke up and sat at the table to eat breakfast with my cousins. Over in the corner of the room, my aunt sat talking on the phone. About a half hour into her conversation, she motioned for me to come over to the phone. "Chaunté, it's for you," she said while handing me the receiver.

Thinking it was my mom, I picked up the receiver and said, "Hi, Mom," waiting to hear her familiar voice on the other end. To my surprise, I did hear a familiar voice, but it wasn't my mom.

"Hi, Chaunté, this is not your mom. This is Grandma," she said. Grandma was my mom's mother. She had always been there for our family my entire life. I was sad when she moved to Riverside to help her brother with his business, but was happy she was in the same city to look after my sisters.

"Oh, I'm sorry. Hi, Grandma," I said, slightly embarrassed by my mistake.

"I'm calling because I think that it's time you move out here with me."

Surprised, I didn't know what to say. It was an obvious choice because I would no longer be alone, but I had no idea what my mom would say. "Can I think about it? I want to talk it over with my mom," I said, not wanting to offend her or seem ungrateful for her offer.

"Sure, you can think it over. But I'll be there in a week, and I need to know by then. You know, sweetie, sometimes you have to make the right decision, even if it's a tough one, to make sure that you are safe and taken care of," she said before sitting silently on the phone.

I already knew what I had to do, but I wasn't sure if I was strong enough to do it. Looking down at my feet, I coiled the phone's cord around my finger. "Grandma?" I whispered. "I'm going to come live with you."

Even knowing I had made the right decision, my heart burned. I felt like I had just betrayed my mom. I'd been waiting all summer, but she hadn't come back for me. School was about to start, and I knew I couldn't wait any longer. At twelve years old, I needed stability. I was now responsible for what I ate, what I drank, and what I wore. I'd leave early in the morning and come back near midnight. I was a mini adult and not a child, and I knew that was not the way it was supposed to be. I knew that my grandma would set boundaries and give me structure, and I would go and get it.

That whole week I stayed in the house near the phone. It had been a couple of weeks since I'd heard from my mom, so I knew she was due to call. Five days passed, and I had not heard from her.

Only a day before I was due to leave, I was afraid my mom's call would come too late for me to get her blessing. That whole night, my stomach turned, and I found it hard to sleep. *What if she doesn't call?* I thought to myself in a panic. Tomorrow morning, I would be moving nearly two hundred and fifty miles away, and I wanted to speak to my mom and hear her approval before I left. Sitting by the phone, I waited the entire night. When I finally gave up, *ring*, the phone jangled loudly across the room.

Before the phone could ring a second time, I picked it up. "Hello, Mom?" I said, hoping dearly that it was her.

"Hey, sweetheart. How are you doing?" I heard my mom say from the other side of the receiver. What should have ended up being a sigh of relief instead caused my fingertips to shake uncontrollably. I knew that I was about to break my mom's heart but wanted to take every precaution to see if I was making the correct decision.

"So, when are you coming back to get me?" I said, casting out my last line of hope for us to be reunited.

The other end of the phone went silent before I heard my mom breathe in deeply and say, "Chaunté, I've looked. There is nothing for me."

Tears streamed down my face as I fought back the anger I felt that she had given up on coming back for me. I knew that the hardships had finally won. She had given up on looking for work, finding a job, and coming back for her girls. It appeared that she was no longer willing to fight.

"Mom, I need a stable place to live, so I need to go live with Grandma," I said, unsure if she would be upset with me. Her side of the receiver was quiet. Trying to soften the blow, I continued, "It helps with my Olympic goals and puts me in a better situation to go to college. In Riverside, I'll be able to race against the fastest girls in the state and get faster myself." It was no secret that the talent in Southern California track and field always impressed, resulting in national headlines annually. I continued, "If I want to be the best, I have to train with and run against the best."

Taken aback by my assertiveness, she questioned, "So you're just going to tell me what you are going to do?"

Even though I wanted to retreat from my boldness, I decided to stay firm in my stance. "Mom, I wish that you were here to see me off, but I need to go." Continuing to make my case, I began to draw on many of our earliest shared memories. "Mom, do you remember when I was four, and I said that I wanted to become an Olympian? It's time for me to take steps toward that goal. I need to go to Riverside to run track."

Silence once again fell on the other end of the line.

"What do you think, Mom?" I asked in a soft, gentle voice.

Responding sincerely, she said, "You're right." With my mother's blessing, a calmness fell over me, and I knew for sure I would be starting a new life tomorrow.

Turning from heartbreak to acceptance, my mom began to advise me on what to expect of city life.

"Do not talk to any strangers at all. I don't care if the nice person is asking for help to cross the street, keep it moving, and do not converse with them." Taking this lighthearted advice as an excuse to laugh, I giggled before promising her that I wouldn't talk to strangers.

The next few minutes were filled with *I love you*s and *goodbye*s before I heard the phone ask my mom to deposit more coins. "All right, baby, I have to go now," she said right before I listened to her end of the line go cold. I hung up the phone and silently went to bed. The following day my grandma arrived at 4:00 a.m., and by 6:00 a.m., I was driving down the Pacific Coast Highway to begin my new life.

10

RIVERSIDE, CALIFORNIA

RIVERSIDE WAS AN urban city sixty miles east of Los Angeles. With a population more than ten times the size of Paso Robles, it was no surprise that the dense traffic reduced our car's speed to a slow crawl. With cars lined bumper to bumper, I reflected on how grateful I was that my grandmother had tinted windows and an excellent air conditioner. Even though the summer was coming to an end, it was still well over 100 degrees Fahrenheit outside.

Realizing that we had not eaten yet, my grandma took the opportunity to show me the scenic route. "All right, Chaunté, this is the city!" she said while motioning for me to look out the window. While the buildings were not as impressive as the skyscrapers that I had seen when we passed L.A., I was still wowed by the modern infrastructure leading us into town. Paso Robles prided itself on the preservation of one-hundred-year-old relics and storefronts rooted in nostalgia and historical pride.

Riverside was the exact opposite. Sleek and up-to-date, it was apparent that the city was planned to live in the "now." It was well equipped with city buses, multiple high schools, and complex highway systems, and I could tell Riverside would be an experience like nothing that I had ever known before. My grandma exited the highway to cruise down the back roads. I pressed my face against the window to get a closer look.

Our tires clung to the asphalt as the car wound artfully around the curved road cascading down a rock mountain. Acting as a tour guide, my grandma began to describe the sights as we passed them. "This is Mount Rubidoux, which is a great place for hiking and to watch fireworks during the new year," she explained while keeping her eyes on the road. The tour continued as we descended the steep slope.

We turned left onto a street called University Avenue, and I looked around at the residential neighborhood. Knowing that *university* was another name for *college*, I turned to my grandma and said, "If this street is called University, does that mean that there is a college nearby?"

Smiling, she answered, "Yes, it does. In fact, several miles down this road is the University of California, Riverside, and it is right up the street from where your mom went to high school."

My mind was utterly blown. I had no idea my mom used to live in Riverside. I was so afraid that I would feel far from my mom, but it was the exact opposite. Moving here would allow me to learn about the mystery life that I never knew my mom had. My stomach began to growl as my grandma talked. I tried my hardest to pay attention, but I was starving.

Driving past the downtown area and a few more residential neighborhoods, we finally stopped at a Chinese restaurant. Pulling up to the drive-thru, my grandmother placed the order for both of us.

With a crackle of the speaker, a woman began to speak. "Hello, thank you for visiting us. Can I take your order?" she said before pausing to hear our reply.

Sticking her head out of the car window and squinting her eyes, my grandma said, "Yes, can I please have the dinner portion of orange chicken and fried rice?" before tucking her head back inside and reaching for her wallet to retrieve a ten-dollar bill.

Seeing her reach for money caused me to do the same. Feeling for the black sock tucked deep in the pocket of my backpack, I also retrieved a ten-dollar bill. As we pulled around, I reached out to hand her the money. Turning in my direction to clear room for our food, she was startled to see that I was staring at her, waiting for her to take my money. Through her eyes, I could see her heart sink. Taking my ten-dollar bill and folding it back into my hand, she gently pushed my hand away and said, "I know you've been through a lot, but it's not your job to take care of me. You are here because I am supposed to take care of you."

I didn't know how to accept what she was saying. I had spent the whole year maturing and learning how to be an adult, but now she was telling me that it was okay for me to be a kid. I probably should have said something, but I didn't. Instead, I just sat there confused, not knowing how to respond. After we'd gotten our food, we headed toward what was going to be my new home. Driving back down University Ave., the way that we had come, we drove up to an electronic gate. Pressing a button on her car's sun visor caused the gate to slide open, letting us in.

"Is this where we live, Grandma?" I asked, impressed by the technology and appearance of the apartment complex.

"Yes, this is home sweet home," she said as she beamed with pride. She had done a fantastic job finding us a home. It was beautiful, secure, and easily the most incredible place I had ever lived. After pulling into our assigned parking space, we were faced with another locked gate. This time my grandmother pulled out a key, unlocked the door, and led me up a beautifully decorated stairway. The complex was small, with roughly eight to ten apartments all facing inward toward one another. In the center was a beautiful garden with vines and flowers. It reminded me of the secret garden I had once read about in a book in elementary school.

After climbing the stairs, my grandmother unlocked the front door to our quarters. When she opened the door, I timidly walked in, only to be abruptly overwhelmed with love. This place immediately felt like home. The inside of the apartment was unbelievably clean. I guess that's what happens when there are no kids to mess things up. There were pictures of me at all ages hanging on the walls.

"Grandma, how did you get all these pictures of me?"

Smiling at my enthusiasm for her collages, she said, "I've been collecting pictures of you since the day you were born."

Looking closer, I saw pictures of my cousins, aunts, uncles, and even a few pictures of my mom. It had been so long since I'd had several family pictures in one place, and they somehow made me feel right at home.

"Okay, Chaunté, it's time to see your new room," Grandma said while pointing toward a door just inside the hallway.

I didn't know what to expect as I walked up to the door. Honestly, I would have been happy with anything. I was grateful to have a roof over my head when I was at my aunt's house, but sleeping on the couch in a place of seven people was not ideal. When my eyes reached the inside of the room, I was overwhelmed with emotion. Inside was a white daybed with porcelain floral accents decorating its four corners. There was a dresser filled with essential clothes that I would need. I'm embarrassed to admit it, but for some time, socks and underwear had become a luxury that I was used to going without. I could see now that those days were far behind me. There were more socks, underwear, and undershirts than I had ever personally owned.

In the closet were clothes that were just my size: a few dresses, some shirts, and a couple of pairs of pants. On top of the dresser were a teen-branded perfume, lotion, deodorant, and a few jewelry pieces. On the floor in the inside of the closet were a pair of shoes. Shoes were crucial to me, even though I usually had to settle for whatever kind I could get. In my entire life, I never remembered having more than two pairs of shoes at a time—one pair for church and another pair for everything else.

"Grandma, whose shoes are these?" I said, not believing that there was any way that these shoes could be mine.

"Those are yours, sweetheart," she said, smiling as she took in my reaction to her gifts.

I had never seen shoes like this before. They were white with two different tones of blue artfully placed along their sides. They had a reflective quality that mesmerized me when the light bounced off them. The soles of the shoe were not flat like most of my shoes. They were curved with a wide pad toward the front of the foot and narrow toward the heel. The shoe's tongue read, *Nike*, and there were gorgeous check marks on the side.

Amazed, shocked, and confused, I found it hard to comprehend why this shoe made me feel excited. "What type of shoe is this?" I asked, holding it up to my grandma's face.

Taking the shoe from me and examining it for herself, she said, "Well, this is a running shoe. Seeing that you can't walk anywhere and you're always running and hopping, I figured that this is the best type of shoe for you."

She was right. Up to this point, I didn't even know that there were different shoes for different types of activities, but if there was a shoe made specifically for running, it was the right shoe for me. Looking inside the shoe, I saw a hump that would land right in the middle of my foot. All the shoes I had ever seen were flat inside, so I figured that this difference must have been suitable for running.

"One last question, Grandma. What is this bump in the middle of the shoe for?" I asked.

"Oh, that is for arch support. It's to make sure you don't get injured. It's good for your feet, your knees, and your lower back," she answered.

"Hmm, okay. Thank you, Grandma," I said while nodding my head in agreement with its importance.

Leaving me to explore my room, my grandma went into the kitchen and set our food on the table. After placing my bags in the closet and plopping onto the bed, I put on my new Nike running shoes and joined her. Immediately feeling right at home, I was surprised at how easily I could adjust to everything around me that was completely different and new. After eating, my grandmother got up from her seat, went to the sink, rinsed off her plate, and then went back to the table with a towel and cleaned the place where she'd been eating.

This act seemed like a little thing but stuck out to me because this was the type of structure that I was missing in my life. She didn't tell me to do the same, but by modeling what was expected, I got up and copied her exactly, rinsing my plate and cleaning my space at the table. Being a mini adult in Paso Robles had its perks, but I knew that there were many more little lessons like this that I still needed to learn in order to develop into the type of person that I wanted to be when I grew up.

Looking at the clock, I could hardly believe that it was still early afternoon. "Wow, Grandma, so much has happened today. I think this is the most change that I have ever had in my life in a single day."

"Well, we're not done yet. We have one more stop to make before the day is over," Grandma said in a very sneaky tone.

Getting back into her car, we drove through a neighborhood with tiny wooden houses. The lawns in front of the houses had dying brown grass enclosed in chain-link fences. The windows had what looked like black jail bars mounted over the glass and *Beware of Dog* signs posted nearby. I was scared. Why would my grandma bring me here? Pulling the car into the driveway of one of the houses, she told me to wait in the car while she knocked on the door.

I was terrified. I did not want my grandma to leave me in the car by myself in this sketchy neighborhood. As soon as she got out of the car, I reached my right hand to the door and promptly pressed the button to lock the car. I then slumped down in my seat to ensure that nobody who passed the car could see that I was inside.

Hiding only lasted a short while before my curiosity overtook me. Leaning upward, just a little, I was able to see my grandmother talking to someone inside of a dark doorway. After a short exchange of information, the person I could not see went into the house, leaving my grandmother outside.

After about a minute passed, the screen door of the house swung open with tremendous force. Two large blurry figures flew right past my grandma and down the path-way leading away from the home. Immediately, I noticed they were headed straight for me. Terrified, I scrunched down low in my seat and closed my eyes, grimacing and waiting for an attack. A loud thud sounded on the passenger-side door. Too afraid to open my eyes, I squeezed them tighter, hoping that the intruders would disappear. Persistently, someone else began to bang on my door while the other one ran to the driver's-side door, checking to see if that one would open.

The banging got louder and louder. "Open the door," they shouted relentlessly, trying to get to me. "Chaunté, open the door," they demanded.

Wait, how did they know my name? These people must know me. Opening my eyes, I looked out of the car win-dows to study the faces of my attackers. Yelping in disbelief, I unlocked the door and jumped out of the car as fast as I could. "Tania!!!" I squealed in delight. Leaping into my oldest sister's arms, I wrapped my arms around her neck and would not let go. Running around from the other side of the car, Alexis wrapped her arms around the back of me, hugging us both. For no reason at all, we all started laughing. Holding one another tighter and tighter, we refused to loosen our grip for fear that it would be another year before we were able to see one another again. Suddenly, all our laughter turned into sobs. We cried deeply and uncontrollably, unable to articulate how miserable this year had been for all of us and how much we had missed one another. Leaving us undisturbed, our grandma let us have this moment to ourselves.

When we had cried all the tears that we could cry, we loosened our grip enough to step back and look at one another. It was weird looking at these two teenagers and realizing how much they both had changed. They were gorgeous and well-adjusted to their new city lives. I couldn't help but think about all the time that we had missed with one another.

We talked nonstop for a couple of hours before it was time for me to go home. Each of us was sad that I had to go, but we were happy that we would be able to be in one another's lives now.

I got back into the car, and we all waved goodbye before my grandma backed out of the driveway. The ride home was silent. I laughed at myself for how afraid I'd been of my sisters' neighborhood. It was clear to me that this was my home now. I missed my mom and hoped at some point she would come here and live with us, but I knew with 100 percent certainty that I would never live without my sisters again. I belonged here, growing up with my sisters, in a home where I was allowed to be a kid while being raised to be a responsible adult. Content with the entire day, I looked out the window and took in the sights, and realized I was finally, for the first time in over a year, going to a place that truly felt like home.

11

BACK ON TRACK

THE NEXT COUPLE of years of middle school were boring in the most amazing way. I went to a good middle school and had lots of great friends. I was always busy either doing homework or spending time with my youth group between school and church. My grandma's big brother was the pastor of our church, and a large portion of the congregation were my family members. One of my mom's first cousins was our Sunday school teacher, and I had more third cousins than I could count.

I did my work and got good grades at school, earning myself a spot on the honor roll almost every semester. Each night, I had a warm meal prepared for me, a stable roof over my head, and not a care in the world. I missed my mom but had security and comfort in my new life. I didn't know that there was such a thing as being too comfortable, but I was precisely that. I was so well taken care of that I had almost completely forgotten why I told my mom I was moving down to Riverside in the first place. My life was great, making me feel no real urgency to change it, but the truth was, my future deeply depended on the actions I needed to be taking right now.

At school, I was in a program called AVID, which stood for, Advancement Via Individual Determination. Initially, I didn't understand the program's mission but joined because my new best friend was a part of it. Right after spring break, just before the school year was set to end, we were assigned a project that made me realize how far I had fallen from my original goals and gave me an urgency to get back on track as soon as possible.

Standing in front of the class and holding a large red presentation board, my teacher gave us the directions for our latest assignment.

"Listen up, class," she started, bringing all of us to attention. "This is my favorite project of the year. You are now finishing the eighth grade and will be beginning high school very soon. The next four years of your life will go by at record speed, and what you do with those next four years can set you on the path that you will be on for the rest of your life. For the rest of this school year, we will use this assignment to create the vision for that path."

By this time, she had our attention. Wide-eyed, we all stared at her, wondering what this assignment was going to be and how it would impact the rest of our lives.

"Each member of AVID expects that they will go to college. So, you will each create a vision board about the college that you will attend and all the reasons why."

After she said that, all the rest of her instruction faded to a blurry haze. *Oh my goodness!* I thought to myself. *How could I have forgotten about my college plans?* I was so happy and peaceful now that I had forgotten my plan to ensure that I would not repeat the cycle of poverty in my life. I wanted to go to college and become an Olympian, but during the last couple of years, I had not taken any meaningful steps toward either of those goals.

I was very aware that one day, I would not be able to rest in the comfort of someone else taking care of me and that I would be responsible for taking care of myself. I was also aware that my time to try out for an Olympic team was going to come on some date in the future, whether I was ready for it or not. What I did or didn't do today mattered toward reaching my goals, and I was not working on my plan.

Snapping out of my shock, I walked to the front of the room, grabbed a poster board, and began to research different colleges. Most of the kids in the class worked on their projects while also casually socializing with friends. On the other hand, I worked diligently on this project as though my very life depended on it. Skimming through the mountain of college brochures set up in the front of the class, I began cutting out pictures to place on my poster board. I cut out a college dorm because I wanted to live on campus with all my friends. The next picture I cut out was a dining hall. I probably gave food too much of a priority in my college decision, but I had spent years hungry and never wanted to experience that again, so the school I chose would have to have good food. The next picture I chose was a college football stadium and track. Any school that I selected would have to have a track scholarship program. While life was now much better than it used to be, I knew that it would still be my responsibility to come up with the cash to go to school.

Part of the project was to find out how much it would cost to go to our college of choice. Taking each brochure and flipping to a page labeled *Tuition*, I learned that college could cost anywhere from $15,000 to $35,000 a year.

"Are you kidding me?" I yelled, almost at the top of my lungs over the already loud class. Rushing to my side, my best friend, Ty, came to my desk and asked, "What's wrong, Tae?" *Tae* was what she alone called me.

"Did you know that college can cost over thirty thousand dollars per year and that you have to go to school for four years?!" I panicked, obviously overwhelmed by the price.

"Yeah, girl, I just saw that, too, but my grandpa said that he is going to pay for me to go to school." Knowing my financial situation, she looked down at the ground and away from me before asking, "How will you pay for school?"

"Girl, you know I don't know anyone with that type of money. I am going to have to get a track scholarship." As soon as I said it, I realized that I had never shared with her my goals of becoming an Olympic track star. I rarely talked about myself in my new friendships, trying my best to leave my past in the past. To be a good friend, I focused on getting to know the other person by asking about their hopes and dreams and burying mine.

With my future on the line, I fessed up and told her. "I want to run track in college and earn a spot on the US Olympic Team."

"Wow, that's cool. Well, I am going to join the cheer team at Clark Atlanta University. So, find a school near Atlanta," she said, making sure that I knew she wanted our paths to remain intertwined.

"You got it!" I agreed, enjoying the idea that I would not have to attend college alone.

After school, as I sat at home on the couch, I realized that I would need to start taking steps toward my Olympic track dreams today. Sitting next to me in her rocking chair, my grandma watched *Jeopardy!*, trying her best to answer the trivia questions before the contestants.

"Hey, Grandma, would it be okay if I worked a summer job this year? I need money to run track in high school."

Not putting up much of a fight at all, she nodded her head yes. "Sure, if that's what you want to do, I'll support you." I loved my grandma. She wasn't a helicopter parent, but I always knew that I could count on her whenever I needed her.

That summer, I executed exactly what I'd planned. I worked a summer job, earned money, and, after buying school clothes, saved five hundred dollars to pay the fee to get on the high school track team. I had not yet met the high school coach or any of the team's members but vowed that I would never again be excluded from sports because of lack of money.

As the summer wound down to an end, we enjoyed the last barbecue at my grandmother's younger brother's house before school was set to begin. My uncle Marvin was hilarious. He was the reason that my grandmother had moved to Riverside in the first place. He owned a business that transported patients in need to and from their medical appointments and employed my grandmother to help him run the business.

I loved going over to his house. He made the best barbecue in the world and spent most of his time telling me fart jokes. As I sat in the corner of the back porch eating my third plate of soul food, I licked my fingers and drove my fork deep into my mound of homemade mac and cheese.

After walking over to me, Uncle Marvin stooped low and whispered in my ear. "Hey, Chaunté, what do you get when you fart on a wallet in your back pocket?"

Bursting out in laughter, I spit out some of my food before grabbing my napkin and wiping my mouth. The whole situation was hilarious to me, and I laughed before I even heard the punchline of his joke. I got a kick out of watching a sixty-year-old man act like a six-year-old schoolboy. "I don't know, what do you get?" I said, eager to hear the punchline.

"You get gas money," he said before laughing hysterically at his own joke. I laughed, too, even though his jokes were kind of corny.

Grabbing his plate and sitting in the chair beside me, he set all jokes aside and started asking me about my plans for the future. "So, you're going to high school next year. How do you feel about it?" he said, tearing the meat off a rib bone with his teeth while looking into my eyes intently.

"I'm excited because I'm going to try out for the track team," I said before taking a large forkful of potato salad and shoveling it into my mouth.

Nodding his head in approval, he licked the barbecue sauce off his fingertips. "Oh, so you're ready to join the family business," he said as a matter of fact.

What's he talking about? I thought to myself. As far as I knew, wanting to run track was a completely original idea, and I was the only person on this side of my family to attempt pursuing it. "What do you mean, family business?" I questioned, thinking he may not have heard me correctly.

"Oh yeah, girl. Running track is in your blood. In fact, your grandma ran track, and she was fast too," he said with a smirk on his face.

"Wait, which grandma?" I questioned, knowing that there was no way that Grandma Bea could have ever run track. My grandma was a very girly girl. She did sweat from time to time, but it was always against her will. She was funny and always laughed but would never approve of the fart jokes that my uncle and I shared. I could not imagine her playing a sport.

"Did you know that your grandma still holds track records at her high school, and your second cousin Dwayne still holds records at your new school? Believe it or not, I used to run track too."

I had no clue that I had come from a long line of at least three generations of track runners.

"Uncle Marvin, I'm not sure I believe you because you're always pulling my leg," I confessed as I finished the last bite of food on my plate. It was hard for me to imagine my now jolly uncle young and fit and running track.

"All right, if you don't believe what I'm telling you, let me show you." Getting up from his seat, he motioned for me to follow him into the house. We walked down the long hallway adorned with family pictures to his living room, where he pulled a photo album from a bookshelf and sat down in his recliner to open it. Searching the pages, he came across the picture he was looking for. Stepping close to him, I peered over his shoulder to get a better look. Within the white borders of a pale image, I saw a boy with an Afro wearing a track uniform. The word *North* was printed across his top, and he was running a race on a dirt track.

"Who's that?" I asked, utterly shocked by what I was looking at.

"This is your second cousin Dwayne, running at the high school that you will be going to next year," he said before thumbing through more pictures. One after another, he showed me pictures of himself, my cousins, uncles, and aunts running track. He was not pulling my leg. Running track was indeed part of my family culture.

That night I couldn't sleep. I was pumped that I would be carrying on a family tradition to run track and knew that I didn't want to wait another day to begin to make my dream of becoming an Olympian a reality. The following day would be the first time I would meet my teachers at the high school's open house. I knew that I had to find a way to get on the dirt track for myself and stand where my ancestors had taken their marks and raced for glory.

Back home, after finally drifitng off to sleep, the morning seemed to come quickly. Greeted by the rays of the sun peeking through the cracks between the blinds, I squinted my eyes before stretching my arms and yawning widely. Nine a.m. couldn't come soon enough. I was in a rush to get to the school and meet my teachers.

As soon as we arrived on campus, my grandmother stopped by the front office and checked us in. After getting my schedule from my counselor, we went from class to class and met each of my teachers. It was exciting, but I had business to attend to. I was on a mission to find the person who held my destiny in their hands.

Clutching the purse at my side, I walked over to my grandmother and whispered in her ear, "Hey, Grandma, do you mind if I walk down to the track?"

"Sure, I don't mind. I need to stay here and fill out all the paperwork for you. Just make sure that you are back in twenty minutes."

Not wanting to waste a single second, I ran to the track. After building up the anticipation of this moment in my head, I was disappointed to find the track empty. Nobody was running or skipping around doing drills. Not a single person was coming out of running blocks or leaping over hurdles. I was disappointed but undeterred from going through with my plan to get on the track team.

Searching every square foot of the dusty dirt oval, I spotted a man who seemed to be counting his footsteps on the track, marking his progress as he went. He had dark skin like mine, a thick mustache, and wore retro sunglasses. Not wanting to interrupt his train of thought, I stood nearby and waited for him to finish.

Aware of me standing there, he finished counting, marked his steps, and then approached me to see what I needed.

"Hello, young lady. How can I help you?" he said, peering down at me through his glasses.

"Hello, sir, my name is Chaunté Howard, and I would like to try out for the track team," I told him assertively. Though it didn't show on the outside, I was trembling with fear on the inside. The sting of rejection still haunted me from the harsh treatment I had received from that soccer coach so many years ago. Clutching my purse, I stopped talking to give him time to respond.

Looking me up and down, just like the soccer coach did, he stopped at my eyes before saying, "Well, okay, then. Runners on my team must run cross-country. Tryouts start right here after school on Monday."

Nodding my head in agreement, I didn't allow myself to feel relief yet, because there was still another obstacle to overcome. Clutching my purse, I grimaced as I asked, "How much does track cost? I have money but want to make sure that I have enough."

Giving me a little scoff before he laughed, he said, "You don't need to pay to be on my team; you just need to come out here and work hard. If you make the team, we have a fundraiser where everyone will work together to cover the costs needed to participate on the team. I'll give you fifty letters for you and your parents to ask fifty people you know for ten dollars. The goal is for each team member to raise five hundred dollars, but nobody will be cut from the team because they can't pay. We'll work it out."

I was overjoyed. I couldn't believe my ears. Not only was I going to get a chance to try out for the team, but I didn't have to spend my money right away. I could either save the money or spend it on something else that I needed.

Thanking him for his time, I walked back up the concrete hill toward my grandmother. Replaying everything he said in my mind, I realized that I had failed to clarify one crucial detail. Making my way back to the track, I once again found my soon-to-be-coach and yelled out, "I forgot to ask, what is cross-country? Does that mean we're going to run across the country over ditches and in the woods?"

Laughing at me again, he said, "Something like that. There will be a lot of running. Just make sure that you have some good running shoes."

Smiling so widely that my cheeks slightly burned, I ran back up the hill, knowing that on Monday, I would officially be back on track for my dreams. When I met up with my grandmother, I could see that she had just finished completing my registration papers.

"You look happy. Where did you go, Chaunté?" she said while packing up her belongings and placing her pen back into her purse.

"I just made the track team," I said, completely ignoring the fact that I still had to try out. In my mind, I had already made the team. If I could earn a spot, then I was going to be on the team. I made up my mind that no matter how hard the training was, there was nothing that my coach could ask of me that I would not do. I was ready to work hard and go after my dream with everything that I was capable of. Monday was day one of the journey that would take me to the rest of my life.

12

TRACK TEAM TRYOUTS

THE ANTICIPATION OF tryouts caused the weekend to go by fast. Several girls of all different sizes, ages, and grades huddled together in running clothes waiting for Coach Leathers to come down to the track. I was confused about the look of fear in their eyes because all I felt was excitement. My moment had finally come, and I believed that I was ready.

Leaning over to the girl closest to me, I decided to find out what was up. I whispered, "Hey, why does everyone look nervous?" I said, hoping to get an answer.

"Oh, you must not know about Coach Leathers. He's tough. Today's workout will be one of your hardest because it is designed to make people quit," she said, also whispering with a look of fear in her eyes.

That didn't make any sense to me. Why would a coach want people to quit the team on the first day? Another girl, who was obviously an upperclassman and who seemed to be the leader, chimed in. "We are a team that is used to winning, and we want to find the runners who want to win with us," she said before stepping out to address the whole group. "All right," she yelled, getting everyone's attention. "Here he comes. If you're afraid to work hard, leave now."

Surprisingly, a couple of people fell into the temptation of going down the easy road and gathered their belongings and left. I couldn't believe that they were giving up without even trying to make the team. The scare tactics did not get to me at all. I'd watched a lot of Disney Channel at home and had seen this story line play out before. A person would act like a drill sergeant, trying to scare the cadets into quitting. It was usually all a ruse toward the end, and the one who remained standing without giving in to fear was a winner.

I believed that the rumored difficulty of this tryout was grossly exaggerated. I was smiling and feeling clever that I'd figured out this game. I sat quietly, listening for the rest of the directions, knowing that there was nothing the coach could say to make me quit.

"All right, girls, anyone who finishes this workout today will make the team," the coach said matter-of-factly.

I knew it, I thought to myself as he continued to give us instructions.

"You have ten 400-meter runs and one hour to complete them." Before Coach could even finish, I laughed loudly, thinking that it was a joke. Embarrassed, I realized that no one else laughed with me. Immediately cutting my laughter short, I quietly stood at attention.

I liked to run, but that workout seemed impossible. Four hundred meters is precisely one time around the track. The most that I had ever run at one time was one mile, and today this coach was asking me to run two-and-a-half-miles' worth of 400-meter runs.

Realizing that I was caught up in my own thoughts, I tuned back in to pay attention to the coach's direction.

"These runs are not walks, and they are not jogs. They are runs, so I expect you to run them. You are more than welcome to quit, but only those who finish will be on the team. I consider walking quitting. Are there any questions?"

I was completely wrong. These were not scare tactics. Our tryout was going to be hard. These girls were afraid, and this monster of a workout was standing between me and my Olympic dreams.

I decided, right then and there: No matter what, I would finish the workout. Walking our group past the track toward the edge of our school's property, Coach Leathers offered no encouragement or instruction. Wanting to see what each of us was made of, he merely said, "It's up to you."

Lining up against the back fence near the road, I saw that these runs were meant to be run on a grass straight at the edge of our school sports fields.

I lined up near the girl who appeared to be the team's leader. I figured if she was the leader, she would most definitely finish the workout and make the team. It was logical that if I stuck close to her and did exactly what she did, I would make the team.

Standing near our start line, the coach held one hand with a stopwatch in the air. With the other hand, he held a whistle to his mouth and blew.

"Set, *FWEET*!" He blew the whistle and lowered his arm. At the sound of his whistle, every runner took off running at a speedy yet comfortable pace. Tucking in to the group to the left shoulder of my target, I matched her foot pattern stride for stride. Relaxed and breathing easy, we finished our first run, and to my surprise, I was not tired at all.

Turning around and walking back, I heard someone ask, "Are you quitting already?"

Realizing that they were talking to me and wanting to set the record straight, I said, "No, I'm just walking back to the start."

When I said that, several of the older girls laughed, and then the one I was following chimed in. "Girl, you don't have time to get back to the line. We only have one hour. Come on, we're going again in ten seconds."

Not able to catch my breath, the couple of minutes that passed might as well have been a couple of seconds. Without a full recovery, my oxygen-deprived legs felt heavy and swollen. My chest started to burn with a tingling warmness, and the air felt thick as I breathed it in. The rays of the sun intensified on my face as beads of sweat began to gather on my forehead. I couldn't believe the pain that I already felt on the second run. Still able to control my limbs, I looked to my target and forced my body to match her stride once again. After finishing the run, I realized that I felt substantially more tired than I did after the first run.

After a couple of moments of rest, it was time to run again. The majority of the pack was still intact, but I noticed that a couple of the girls began to fall off, taking their belongings and quietly exiting the track. Determined not to quit, I stuck next to my target, doing my best to ignore the fatigue that I was feeling.

With each run, the pain of hard work intensified, causing more girls to quit the tryout. By run six, more than half of the girls were gone. For me, the pain was constant. The few moments of rest offered little to no relief as I knew the next run was coming to force my body to do something that it did not want to do. Runs seven, eight, and nine caused me to pep talk my body in my mind.

All right, Chaunté, you can do this. These girls are flesh and blood, just like you. Which means you can do it if they can do it. The pep talk worked. No matter how hard the runs got, I was able to put one foot in front of the other and finish. When the tenth run came, I realized that I was almost at the finish line and was surprised by a sudden burst of energy. I was excited because I knew that I would be on the team if I made this run.

Lining up along the start with the few girls who were left, I waited for someone to yell, "Set, GO." When I heard it, I sprinted off the line as fast as I could. Surprised by my effort, a couple of the girls tried to match my pace before giving up and falling behind. The girl that I had been targeting all along was now matching my pace stride for stride before she sprinted past me to reach the finish line first. When I reached the line, she held her hand up and gave me a high five.

"Wow, girl. You got out on that one."

Too exhausted to talk, I was only able to smile and nod before lying flat on my back, attempting to let my body recover finally. Standing over me and reaching her hand out, the girl I had been targeting stooped down to help me up.

"Get up, girl, we don't do that after a workout. You're one of us now. I'm your team captain, Nicole," she said while walking me back toward the entrance to the track. My body felt tired, but on the inside, I beamed with pride. That workout was brutal, and I had finished. Many girls had quit, but I hadn't, and now I was officially on JW North's track team and was one step closer to being an Olympian.

In terms of difficulty, the next three weeks were almost as intense as the first day. The training was brutal, and I wondered if I was cut out for the goals that I had set for myself. We'd come to the track, warm up together, and then as a group would complete the most challenging work-outs we'd faced in our entire lives.

Each day, building on the one before, the fight to stay on the team became more of a mental battle than a physical one. I wasn't used to the pain of getting in shape, and at the time, I felt like I was in a customized brand of torture. Every part of my body was sore and stiff, and even walk-ing felt like a demanding chore. Sitting through classes was tough, and I asked the teacher if I could have permission to stand at the back of the class instead of learning from my desk.

Out of nowhere, when I could not imagine a foreseeable end to the difficulty of practice, the pain began to dull and subside. By the end of week three, even though the workouts were still hard, the achiness subsided until I couldn't feel it anymore. What was once daily torture was replaced with strength and endurance.

Throughout cross-country season, I got faster and stronger alongside the rest of my team. None of us liked long, slow running because we were all sprinters at heart. However, we all did it with the common goal of being California State Track and Field Champions by the end of the year.

13

HIGH-JUMP GLORY

WHEN CROSS-COUNTRY SEASON was finally over, we were all excited to get into our event-specific training. Track and field is made up of several different disciplines focused around the three basic skills of running, throwing, and jumping. Up to this point I didn't know what events I wanted to do but I would need to figure it out soon. My fascination with the Olympics started with me seeing FloJo fly out of the starting blocks as a powerful sprinter. So naturally, sprinting was where I thought I would land.

As I walked down the track, buzzing with excitement, I was accompanied by the two other freshmen who had made the varsity team.

"Hey, Tracee, which track events are you going to compete in this year?" I said, wondering if we would be in the same specialty group.

"I'm going to run the 100, the 200, and probably the short relay," she said with a clarity that I didn't have. Tracee was well trained in track and had been running in organized track since she was seven years old. "What about you? What events are you going to do?" she asked, while putting down her bag and tightening her laces before we ran our warmup laps.

"I'm not sure. I'll probably run the 200 and the 400," I said, while also setting my school bag down and joining her for the jog around the track. As we turned around the last curve and headed toward the last straight to finish our lap, I saw a group of kids I didn't know pulling out a jumbo-size red mattress from gated storage units positioned under our school's pool.

I recognized those mats to be high-jump landing pads. I'd seen them before when I was in middle school. During PE, when we were doing a unit on sports exploration, I was able to try high jump on track-and-field day. I remembered that I was good at it and had beaten everyone, including the boys, with a jump of four feet and seven inches.

Now unable to focus, I couldn't take my eyes off the small group setting up for high-jump practice. "Hey, Tracee, did you know that we had a high-jump team?" I questioned.

"No, I don't think that any of our high jumpers made it to the CIF championships last year. So that's probably why I didn't know about them."

As we began our second lap, I identified a bald man who I had seen around campus, but never on the track. He seemed to be the high-jump coach. So instead of doing my lap with my friends I stopped to talk to him.

"Hey, are you the high-jump coach?" I said trying to find a smooth way to introduce myself.

"Yes, I'm Coach Robert and I coach all the jumps," he said, without taking his eyes off his setup operation.

"Well, I jumped once in middle school and want to high-jump here too," I said, hoping that he would be delighted to have another jumper.

"Oh yeah, what's your best jump?" he asked, now stopping and taking a moment to size me up.

"Well, I jumped four feet, seven inches and beat all the boys and girls in my school," I bragged.

"Nope, go over to Coach Leathers; we have enough jumpers," he said, shooing me away.

Walking away irritated, I couldn't believe that he didn't even give me a try. Refusing to be dismissed without getting a chance to prove myself, I decided that I was not going to give up. Every day, I would do the same exact thing. I'd run my warm-up laps and each time I went around I would shout out to him, trying to convince him that he wanted me on his team.

"Hey, Coach Robert, let me jump!" I yelled from the track without breaking my stride.

"No, Chaunté, go run with your group and leave me alone," he said, like he'd done every time I'd asked him before.

"Haha! He knows my name now. I guess I'm wearing him down," I chuckled to myself, still encouraged that I could get a spot on the jump squad.

One Friday, after weeks of annoying Coach Robert to no end, I decided to challenge him. "You know what, Coach Robert? I've seen your girls practice, and I bet you I can beat every one of them. So, if you don't want me to jump for you, you are the one missing out."

I didn't know where all this unearned confidence came from, but I had it and I wasn't going to ignore it.

Apparently, he couldn't ignore it either because he laughed hysterically before addressing my claims directly. "Yeah, right. Some of these girls have been training with me for three years, and you think that you can beat them all. Challenge accepted. After practice come over here and if you can beat all my jumpers, you can be on the team," he said, hoping to humble me and finally put an end to my relentless harassment.

All throughout sprint practice I ran hard but remained distracted. My gaze kept drifting over to the high-jump area, where the jumpers were sharpening their skills. Their training seemed to be going well, because every so often I would hear high shrieks as a jumper would clear the bar, while the other jumpers and the coach looked on and cheered. Bar after bar, they would raise the height and cheer, setting new personal-best records along the way.

On the other side of the track, I was being handed a very taxing sprint workout. I was tired and trying to conserve energy for the competition that I had after practice. That didn't work with Coach Leathers. He had a talent for knowing when you were not giving a full effort in training, and a greater talent for pulling the best out of every run. I had no choice. Today I was going to have to do both. I needed to give this workout my very best and, also, dig down deep and access my inner warrior to jump higher than every other girl on my team.

I did it! Finishing the last run of our workout, I stooped over the grass on the infield of the track and caught my breath before making a direct beeline for the high-jump pit. As I walked up, I noticed there was a medium-size crowd gathered, when there usually was not. I felt like I was walking into a schoolyard fight.

"Oh, here she comes. You better show her what you've got," someone said while random "Oohs" came from different voices all around me.

Oh wow! I thought to myself. *First, who invited all these people, and second, how dare they assume that I am going to lose?* Their doubt fired me up. I was so excited to prove them wrong and become our team's best high jumper. I understood the odds weren't particularly in my favor. My legs were tired from a hard workout, and the athletes that I would be competing against had been practicing this event for years. I didn't care about any of that in this moment. My ego was the size of Texas, and I was about to literally jump into my destiny.

Making me attempt the first clearance, the coach set the bar at four feet. Not having a mark or knowing where to stand, I jogged back a couple of steps, ran as fast as I could to the bar in a straight line, and jumped as high as I could. I cleared the bar easily, but so did the other girls.

"Okay, I see that you came to play. I'm going to reverse the order so now you will be jumping last," the coach said before raising the bar another four inches to four feet and four inches. Already I could see the differences in the way that I jumped versus the other jumpers. Each of them had a measured mark to take off from and approached the bar in a J motion. While I stood straight up and jumped over the bar kicking my legs in a scissor motion, the other girls jumped backward over the bar like a back flip. They were well polished in their technique, and I was not.

The bar now looked much higher, but I refused to dwell on all the reasons why I couldn't clear it and convinced myself of all the ways that I could. As I waited for my turn to jump again, I watched the other girls closely and knew that I would have to try my best to even the playing field.

When it was my turn for my second jump, the bar was at four feet, four inches. "Okay, Chaunté, it's up there. Let's see what you got," Coach Robert said while whispering in his top jumper's ear. I stood at my mark, ran up to the bar, and jumped as high as I could in the air. Not a single part of my body touched the bar. As soon as I landed on the mat safely, a loud roar erupted from all the onlookers standing by. As the yelps and squeals got louder, the size of the crowd seemed to grow.

Out of the five jumpers I was competing against, only four were able to clear this height. *All right, Chaunté,* I thought to myself. *One down and four to go.* Seemingly unmoved by the crowd, I looked at no one and talked to no one, only stared at the bar intently as the coach once again raised it another four inches.

"Okay, Chaunté, what do you got?" the coach playfully taunted. "Remember, once you lose, you can't bother me about high jumping anymore."

Finally saying something that struck a nerve with me, I looked at him and said, "Sorry, no such luck. Get used to being bothered because losing is something that I just don't do." Not even waiting for his response, I went back to a starting point and ran full speed at the bar. Still doing a stand-up jump, I cleared the bar and set a new personal best in the high jump of four feet and eight inches. All but one of my competitors were unable to match this height.

Chuckling to myself, I murmured under my breath, "Tell me what else I can't do so that I can keep proving you wrong." Now, when I looked at the coach, he had a big smile on his face. For him this was a win-win situation. If I lost, I would finally stop annoying him about being part of his group. If I won, he would have acquired an amazing jumper. I preferred the latter but knew I was going to have to adjust for that to happen.

As the bar was now very high, the coach raised it only two inches instead of four. I was jumping first, and the other girl was going to follow me. This time I went back to a different mark, situating myself at a spot where I too could run a J-shaped approach. I stood at my new mark, ran as fast as I could, and in a last-minute decision decided to jump backward over the bar instead of straight up, like I had the entire competition. Instead of sailing over the bar like I had done so many times before, I crashed right into it, causing the bar to topple to the ground.

That was so dumb. Why did I do that? I thought as I watched my win slip out of my grasp. At four feet and ten inches, the other girl went to her mark the same way she had done every single jump and ran up to the bar. To my surprise, she too caused the bar to come crashing to the ground. At this point Coach Robert was smiling ear to ear. Walking over to me he said, "Okay, Chaunté, now is not the time to try a technique that you have never practiced. Go back to your old way of jumping and give it another try."

Going back to my original mark, I intended to do just that. "Okay, Coach Robert, I am sure I can make this height on my second try," I said before taking a deep breath and getting ready to go.

"Oh no, I'm not going to make it that easy," he said through a grin as he went up and raised the bar two more inches.

"Oh my gosh, I think that is the school record," I heard a boy say, causing me to look at the crowd. I couldn't believe my eyes. The crowd that had gathered was massive. Students from several different sports had come over to watch the excitement and see if I could indeed beat all our current jumpers. Hearing the crowd and seeing the faces of my peers did something inside of me. I wanted to perform for them and give them a show. Completely fearless, I went to my mark and ran to the bar. Stamping my left foot into the ground, I propelled myself up into the air as high as I could. I cleared the bar by what seemed like a mile.

"Yes, just like that," Coach Robert said, before running up to me and giving me a high five. The other girl also applauded before getting to her mark and running toward the bar. She also stamped her foot deep into the ground, but the bar came crashing down. With a sigh of relief, I knew exactly what that meant. I was the team's new best high jumper and I could now bother Coach Robert as much as I wanted.

I walked up to the other jumper and extended my hand. "You did a great job and I look forward to us working together."

Smiling back at me, she high-fived me and said, "This is going to be a lot of fun."

Taking a minute to reflect on what had just happened, I realized that I had never felt like this before. Facing new challenges, hearing the roar of the crowd, and pushing myself to new heights was amazing. I liked winning and it was something I planned to experience repeatedly. From that day forward I was officially classified as a high jumper, and I couldn't have been more thrilled. The goal was the same: I would go to the Olympics when the time was right, but instead of hurtling down the track at record speed, I would be propelling into the air as high as I could, and breaking records before I came down.

14

COLLEGE SCHOLARSHIP

WITH TWO YEARS of high school track now under my belt, it was easy to see high jump was a natural fit for me. Now, splitting my time between the jumping and sprinting groups, I had to work twice as much as everyone else to make sure that I was ready for both. However, the extra work didn't bother me because my expectations for myself were high, and my goals were lofty.

Now in my junior year of high school, everything seemed to be going exactly as I'd planned. Having climbed my way up to becoming one of the top 400-meter runners on our team, I earned a spot on the mile relay. Our relay team was recognized nationwide and was often invited to fly to national championship meets to compete with America's best.

The winning culture was now well established and interwoven into our DNA. Like robots, we trained hard, competed, and won. Not everyone was cut out for this type of work, which resulted in our tiny core group of girls. Not having many competitors meant we were expected to specialize in two to three events and participate in the relays.

Everyone on my team had started running competitive track several years earlier and knew exactly where they fit. On the other hand, I had only been running in an organized setting since my freshman year of high school and had just gotten the hang of several new events. The high jump was the only event where I ranked among the best in the States. Triple Jump was an event that I had just begun learning, and I felt with more practice, I'd have a chance of winning points for our team in the state championships.

Having just finished my third cross-country season, I was so excited to finally get back to track work and develop my skill in another event. Coach Leathers and Coach Robert had worked out a schedule to determine the amount of time I would spend with each training group. Mondays were the days I was with Leathers and usually included the gut-wrenching training that required physical and mental strength.

As I walked down to the track and placed my bag at our usual spot, I was met by both coaches, which was unusual. "Hi, Coaches, is there a problem?" I said, nervous that I had done something wrong.

Coach Leathers was the first to speak. "No, nothing is wrong. This is about what is going right." Still confused, I had no idea where this conversation was going.

Coach Robert chimed in to help clarify the purpose of this conversation. "You are doing amazing in the high jump, and we believe that you can win State in that event this year."

Now smiling from ear to ear, I loved the direction that this conversation was taking.

While experimenting with other events, I felt ownership over the high jump. The idea of winning the state title was an honor that I wanted. I chose not to interject and instead nodded my head up and down in agreement. This conversation was the one that I had been waiting for. I was sure that they were about to tell me which other events we would be putting our focus on. However, that is not what happened. Instead, the conversation took an unexpected and horrible turn.

"We have been talking and have decided that for you to have the best chances of getting a full scholarship to college, you need to give up all your other events and focus solely on the high jump this year," Coach Robert said as Coach Leathers nodded in agreement.

No longer able to keep silent, I interjected. "NO! Why would you decide that I can't do all the events? Would you please give me a chance?"

"I'm sorry, Chaunté, this is not up for debate. My goal is to get you a full scholarship, and this is the best way," Coach Leathers said, now taking the lead in the conversation.

My arms crossed, I wanted to throw a tantrum like a toddler but knew this would get me nowhere. "That doesn't make any sense. Why would doing fewer events make colleges want me more?" I immediately regretted my attitude. Up to this point, Coach Leathers had sent dozens of girls to college on full scholarship, including several who'd competed in the Olympic Trials. He deserved my respect and for me to hear him out. Uncrossing my arms, I controlled my attitude and listened to his reasoning.

"Everyone thinks an athlete's senior year performance is the main focus of college recruiters, but that is not true. The recruiting window will open the summer after your junior year. That means that your chances of earning a scholarship will depend on the performances you put up this year. I know you don't want to hear it, but in the high jump, you are good, but you are not yet great. We must get you great and to do that, we need you to focus on the high jump alone."

Now crying, I knew that he was right. I had finished top three in the state meet but was only top twenty on the national list. When it came to scholarships, I knew that I would be competing against every other girl in the nation, and my performance was just not where it needed to be to guarantee me a completely free education.

Submitting to my coach's authority and wisdom, I decided to make one last request before working toward being the best high jumper in the nation. "Once I earn the scholarship and sign with a school, can I please do all my other events again?"

"Absolutely, if you earn a scholarship, you can do whatever events that you want," Coach Leathers said before walking away and leaving me with Coach Robert.

Over the next couple of months, Coach Robert and I worked hard and consistently. We scrutinized every detail of the high jump and perfected it. Taking away all excuses, we held ourselves to the highest standard of performance and no longer solely focused on the win, but the height of the win compared to every other girl jumper in the United States. I started training with boys to push myself at practice because they were taller and stronger than I was. I was glad that I didn't have to compete against them for a scholarship but was happy to use their ability to push me to a higher level of performance.

Our plan worked. Our first test came indoors with the L.A. Invitational. I won that meet fast and easy with no real competition. My indoor performances opened the door to being invited to the most prominent track festival in the

United States. I was so excited to go to this meet because I would get to see Nicole again. She had gotten a full scholarship to the University of Texas and would be at the meet competing for her college team.

Getting on the plane and flying across the country was a dream come true. The University of Texas was a great school that always competed for national championships. When we arrived at the hotel, we were greeted by Nicole, my former team captain and old friend from my high school! The same Nicole who challenged me to work so hard during my tryout on the first day of high school track. I was so proud of her for earning a scholarship to college and for thriving in that environment. Coach Leathers and Nicole's new coach were friends, and they went off to the side to talk like adults while the rest of us took the opportunity to ask Nicole about college life.

"So, what's it like being in college?" I asked, eager to see it through her eyes.

"It's awesome. You get to live with your best friends, be part of a winning team, and go to one of the best schools in the nation."

Hearing her experience from her eyes had me hooked. No longer did I just want to go to college, but I wanted to be a Texas Longhorn.

Coach Leathers came over to make an announcement. "After the meet, Nicole's coach is having a barbecue at her house, and she invited a few of us to come to hang out." Thinking back to the barbecues at my uncle Marvin's, I smiled, imagining all the excellent food.

Before we left the lobby, Coach Leathers yelled out to me, "Hey, Chaunté, let me talk to you for a minute." He motioned me over to a place where we were out of earshot of the other girls. "I talked to the coach about what it would take for a high jumper to get a full scholarship, and she said she wouldn't take anyone who jumped less than six feet."

"Wait, what?!" I scoffed. "How is that possible? Number one, I am the highest jumper in the nation right now, and number two, there is only a handful of women in college who have better marks than me," I said, not believing what I was hearing. "Does she know that?" I asked, hoping to get a better understanding of her ill-advised standards.

"I'm not sure if she does, but what I want you to do is win that meet tomorrow and show her that you are the jumper who she wants," he said, devising a plan to help me earn a scholarship.

"Okay, I can do that, but I will also talk to her at the barbecue and let her know more about high-jump performances," I said, devising a plan of my own.

"About that; you were one of the ones who were not invited," he said reluctantly, while putting his head down. I was livid and took the lack of invitation as the most profound sign of disrespect. Only six of us had traveled on this trip, and one of the other girls was a freshman and wouldn't be going to college for several years.

I probably shouldn't have held a grudge, but I did. I jumped in the Texas relays the next day and won, jumping five feet eleven inches, and extending my national lead. As soon as I'd finished jumping, my coach came up to congratulate me and give me some good news.

"Hey, Chaunté, you did a good job today. So much so that you caught the attention of the Texas coach. She would like to invite you to her house for the barbecue."

I couldn't believe my ears, yet I wasn't surprised at all. I knew how hard I had been training, and I was training to be the best jumper in the nation. I believed in myself and what I was willing to do to get to the top, but it was apparent that she did not. I did not want to reward any bandwagon behavior and chose the low road when crafting my response to her invitation.

"Please tell her that I disrespectfully decline. I will not be going to her house. Can you please take me back to the hotel?"

Completely taken aback by my response, my coach opened his eyes wide before saying, "Well, I'm not going to tell her that." Then he walked me to our rental van in silence.

I was ashamed of my attitude. I was so focused on defending my honor that I wasn't enjoying my first win at a nationally prestigious invitational. I thought that declining her invitation would make me feel good, but it didn't. Anger and spite made me feel sad and exhausted. So, instead of allowing those feelings to simmer and replay in my head, I let it go and allowed myself to move on emotionally. Pushing the entire situation entirely out of my head, I started thinking about my goals and how I had reached a significant milestone that day in my quest to be recruited to college.

The rest of the year I went on an exhilarating tear, winning every meet I competed in. Ranking number one in the nation was the goal, but we decided that we would not take our foot off the gas until our goal to get me into college was accomplished. Knowing that I could not get into school without good grades, I allowed the standard of excellence that I set for myself to spill over into the classroom as well.

All the hard work was causing me to burn the candle at both ends, which left me tired most of the day. History was the most challenging class for me to pay attention to, and lately, I'd found myself falling asleep during class.

"Chaunté, wake up!" my classmate said while nudging me on the shoulder. Not realizing I'd fallen asleep again, I looked over at the teacher, who was staring at me like she was waiting for me to say something.

"Chaunté, did you hear me? You need to go to the office," she said before hanging up the classroom phone and pointing me out the door. I was disappointed in myself for letting my classroom performance slip as I gathered my things.

I'm just going to have to go to bed earlier, I said to myself, and I imagined all the trouble that I was about to get into. *I'll just tell the principal the truth, that I'm tired because I was not getting enough rest.*

I walked into the office and sat in one of the chairs of doom, waiting to be called back. I gave the secretary my name, and she let me know I would be talking to the school counselor, Mrs. Decker. After a few moments, I was told I could go back.

Once I got into the office, I sat down quietly, waiting for her to speak first. "Do you know why you are here, Chaunté?" she said, staring at me and smiling. Her smile confused me. She didn't have a look on her face that indicated I was in trouble at all.

"Well, I thought I did, but I'm not sure," I said, deciding not to tell on myself for sleeping in class.

Reaching under her desk, she pulled out a large stack of envelopes and handed them to me. "These are for you."

Taking the stack in my hand, I couldn't understand why I was getting mail at school. Each envelope was addressed to me. It wasn't until I was halfway through the stack that I realized what was going on.

Jumping up out of the seat, I yelled at the top of my lungs, "I'm being recruited!" I couldn't believe it. I had letters from Berkeley, Stanford, Harvard, UCLA, and more. My dream was finally becoming a reality. I couldn't wait to get home and tell my grandma.

I was so grateful that it was a Friday and we didn't have practice. These days were rare, but I cherished every one of them. Once I got home, I realized that my grandmother was not there yet. Too excited to relax or go into my room, I sat on the couch and dropped my backpack at my feet in front of me. Reaching into the bag, I fingered through the envelopes again, looking at all my potential universities.

I had waited for this moment for so long and couldn't believe that I was finally here. I had spent so much time thinking about how I would get to college that I forgot to seriously consider the criteria I would use to choose a school.

When I first thought about getting a scholarship to go to college, I had hoped to pique the interest of one school, and now I had ten letters in my hand, all from schools interested in having me on their teams. It wasn't long before my grandma came walking through the door.

"I'm home," she sang as she entered the apartment and unloaded her things on the floor. Too eager to lead her on, I jumped up and held up the letters to her face.

"We did it!" I exclaimed. "I'm being recruited for college."

Though she was happy, it didn't seem like she was surprised at all. "I knew you could do it, Chaunté. Praise God. I am so happy for you," she said, raising her hands in the air and smiling widely. You could tell she expected this to happen eventually, but she was excited about it nonetheless.

"Grandma, my coach said that I will probably get more of these letters and that, more than likely, with my grades and my performance, I will be able to go to whatever school that I want. I have no idea how I will choose a school," I said with worry evident in my voice.

"Okay, sweetheart, you have to think about what you want and go to the school that is most likely to provide it."

This made my choice much more straightforward. I knew exactly what I wanted—I had known that since I was four years old. "I want to be an Olympian and a scholar," I said with confidence.

"All right, then, you want to go to a school that sends people to the Olympics and a school that is academically challenging," she said as she looked at me with pride in her eyes. Being a woman who relied heavily on her faith, she didn't miss the opportunity to bring God into the equation. "Also, don't forget to pray and know that God will lead you in the right direction."

Over the following weeks and months, I was called almost every day to pick up recruiting letters from the office. I delighted in each letter and thoroughly researched each school interested in having me attend. My criteria were simple. First, was it an academically ranked school, and second, had the jumps coach ever sent anyone to the Olympics in the high jump?

Finding this combination was very difficult. Everyone who knew about my dilemma recommended that I go to a school like Harvard or Stanford, but at the time, they had not sent any high jumpers that I'd known to the Olympics. I loved the prestige of those schools, but I needed a school that would address both of my goals.

Finally, in July, I received a call from a coach named Nat Page from Georgia Tech. After having what seemed to be a hundred conversations with different college recruiters, I had learned to get to the point early in the call. I asked only two questions when I spoke with him. "Hi, Coach Page, thank you for calling to see if I would be a good fit for your team. Can you please tell me if your school is academically competitive?" I said.

I could tell he wasn't just telling me what I wanted to hear by the confidence that radiated from his voice. "We were ranked among the top ten schools in the nation last year for our engineering program," he said before asking me to give him my next question.

"Okay, have you ever coached an Olympian in the high jump?" I asked, not expecting the answer to be what I wanted to hear.

"Not only have I coached an Olympian, but my Olympian is also the indoor American record holder in the women's high jump," he said, confident that he'd answered the question correctly.

I'd never gotten to a third question before, but I was ready. "Final question, what event would you have me do if I came there?"

This was an essential question because several teams that recruited me wanted me to either high jump or change my event altogether.

"Well, I would want you to do the high jump, long jump, triple jump, and the hurdles." That was the correct answer.

I had wanted to return to my other events ever since I was convinced to specialize in just the high jump earlier this year.

I was sold. This was the school for me. After agreeing to visit Georgia Tech in Atlanta, I signed a scholarship contract and officially committed to becoming a Yellow Jacket the following fall.

15

COLLEGE DREAM

As THE PLANE approached Atlanta, Georgia, I marveled at the elegantly designed skyscrapers. I couldn't believe that I had finally made it. The first of my two massive life goals was complete. I was now a collegiate student-athlete on a full scholarship. This was a big moment in changing my life's path, and I understood that I needed to take this opportunity seriously. Remembering Granny Booker's words so many years ago, I realized she was right. The path I was on looked completely different now. The life that I lived as a child was not the life I was living as an adult. Once this plane landed, everything would be forever changed, and I would begin day one of charting a new path for my future.

Once the plane landed, I made my way to the Georgia Institute of Technology, where I couldn't wait to connect with Coach Page. He knew that I was arriving and set up some time to meet him in his office. I wasn't sure what we would talk about, but I was excited to hear anything that he had to say. Over the last year, we had gotten to know each other. He called our home often, talking to my grandmother and me, making sure that I would feel at home once I got to the college campus.

He gave us regular updates on the team and would take extra care walking us through the recruiting process. Even though we weren't related, he looked like he could be my natural father, and from the first day we met, I could tell that he cared. He was a nurturing person who was a blast to talk to. He made it a point to let me know that he cared for all his athletes as people first and athletes second. Being nearly three thousand miles away from my home and everything I knew was scary, but knowing that he would be looking out for me was reassuring.

Sitting in his office in a comfy plush chair, I waited for him to come in and start the meeting. When he arrived, he sat at the desk in front of me before clasping his hands and looking at me intently.

"All right, so you made it," he said with a big smile. "I wanted to have this meeting with you because I want to know your goals," he explained, revealing the reason we were both sitting here.

"My goals are simple because they have been the same since I was four years old. I want to become an Olympian," I said with unwavering surety.

"Okay, we can do that, but do you know where you place on the world ranking list?" he said before sitting quietly, allowing me to answer.

"World list?" I asked. "I didn't even know there is a world list. Well, I know I'm number one in the nation for high school and college," I said, wanting to prove that I was at least sort of aware of where I stacked up against my competitors.

"That's an amazing accomplishment, but to become an Olympian, you will be jumping against the world's best," he explained, while shuffling through his bag and pulling out a magazine. "This is the *Track & Field News* magazine and tells you the world rankings of all of the jumpers in all the events. When we go to the women's high jump—and notice I said *women's* and not *girls'*—you can find out your ranking by finding your name."

Taking the magazine from his hands, I examined it in shock. I couldn't believe such a magazine existed. I had no idea that this information was even available or that world rankings could be tracked.

As I looked to find my name, Coach Page continued, "They only print the top fifty jumpers in the world. So, with your jump of six feet, one and a half inches, where are you?"

Starting at the top of the list, I kept going farther down, but I could not find my name. Finally, when I reached the bottom of the list, I found my name printed in the fiftieth spot. This meant that coming out of high school, I was the fiftieth best jumper in the entire world. I was proud of this revelation and began to smile. "My name is in there," I said, smiling and showing my new coach.

"That is great, but it is not enough to make an Olympic Team. If being an Olympian is your goal, then we have a lot of work to do," he said before taking the magazine back from me.

"We only have two years to get right here," he informed me, while pointing to the upper quadrant of the list. "You must qualify for the Olympic Games with a minimum qualifying standard of six feet, four and three-quarters inches. Next, you have to beat out three American professionals at the Olympic Trials to earn a spot on the US team."

I had to admit he was right. Even though I was proud of my accomplishments, we still had a lot of work to do. I'd jumped extremely high for a high schooler but would be competing against professionals for my spot on the US Team, and I was not ready for that yet. Before I could soak in this revelation, Coach Page jumped up and said, "Good. I can see you understand. Now let's go eat."

I could tell that he loved food. Coach Page was a skinny man, but he always talked about eating every time we conversed. Walking out of his office and down a set of stairs, we entered the student-athlete dining hall. The smells of freshly grilled food met us out in the corridor, inviting us to come in and fill our bellies. Looking around, I couldn't believe that the athletes were treated so well.

"Do they do this every day?" I asked, looking over to Coach Page in disbelief.

"Yes, they actually do it three times a day, for breakfast, lunch, and dinner."

Within the dining hall, there were several stations with various types of food. The service was buffet style, so each athlete, coach, and athletic staff member could grab a tray and eat whatever they had a taste for. I'd only eaten at a buffet once or twice before when we went to the Sizzler for my birthday, and I had a hard time understanding the concept of eating as much as you wanted until you were full.

I was never a big eater but loved to taste new and exciting foods. This was probably because of how scarce food had always been when I was a child. Sizzling steam sent the aroma of grilled beef, fish, chicken, and veggies to every corner of the building. Picking up my tray, I went to the seafood station to get grilled fish. "Hello, may I please have a small piece of flounder?" I said to the cafeteria worker after reading the label in front of his station.

"Yes, you may," he replied while placing a healthy portion on my plate.

Examining the large piece of fish, I couldn't help but think about how beautiful it was. Decorated with a bright yellow lemon wedge and peppered with rich green herbs, this meal was pleasing to the eye. Next, I walked to the salad station, building the most beautiful rainbow arrangement of tomatoes, cucumbers, olives, lettuce, and purple onions. At this point, I felt it was best to go to the table and eat, but as I was walking, I was tempted by the ice cream machine. Unable to resist, I grabbed a cone and filled it with soft-serve vanilla ice cream.

I had never eaten like this in my entire life. Right then and there, I decided that I loved college life. Going back to the table, I was afraid that Page would reprimand me for eating ice cream. Instead, he looked at my ice cream, turned his head to the side, and said, "Oh, what a good idea," before getting up from the table to get his own.

His response confirmed to me that I had finally found my place in the world and declared in my mind, *I love college life*.

After lunch, I went across campus to set up my dorm room. The whole experience made me feel like a grown-up. Our dorms were built to house Olympians from the 1996 Atlanta Olympics and were modern and sleek. After walking in the front door, I learned that I would be living in an apartment rather than a shared bedroom-style dorm room like I had seen on TV. We had a shared living room area and kitchen. Each apartment had four bedrooms and two bathrooms, and no one was expected to share a room.

This was beyond my wildest dream. I was living in a house with my teammates while going to school and running track. Walking into my bedroom, I closed the door behind me and dropped to my knees with the ugliest "smile-cry." Remembering the days of sleeping on a stranger's floor or having our belongings thrown out onto the street brought tears to my eyes. Even though I was crying, I was grateful.

"Look how far you have come, Chaunté! You did it, and there is no turning back now," I said, congratulating myself.

Over the next two years, I didn't lose an ounce of enthusiasm toward reaching my dreams. Every day, I went to class, went to practice, and then came home to study. With only two years to improve to world-class performances, I treated each training session, competition, and class lesson like it had the power to make my dreams come true. The hard training was working, and I improved my personal best by two inches. I now ranked among the professional jumpers, but the height was not high enough. I still needed to improve one and one-fourth inches to make the Olympic qualifying standard of six feet, four and three-quarters inches.

After each long week of classes, I'd look to the weekend as a chance to get to the qualifying mark for the Olympics.

This weekend was no different. Almost every track meet seemed to be the same. The bar would start low with several girls representing their colleges. They'd battle it out, and when every girl was out, I would enter the competition and be forced to jump by myself. I assumed that was just a result of where each of us placed our goals. While most girls were focusing on winning titles for their school, my focus since the day that I stepped on the track—and even before then, since I was a young child—was to win titles for our country. I literally wanted to jump out of a life of poverty and was unmoved by merely winning meets. I needed to get to the Olympic Games.

At the ACC championships, my chance to compete in the high jump came early in the competition. Safety-pinning my bib number across my chest, I couldn't help but remember FloJo in 1988. The number across my chest was 195. Realizing this number was symbolic, I took it as a sign that today was the day. I had studied the height that I needed to jump so well that I knew 1.95 meters was the metric equivalent of the height of the Olympic standard.

Standing at my mark, I jumped five feet, ten inches without a miss. I looked at the official and said, "Raise the bar two inches." This was one of my favorite parts of being in the competition alone. Since I was the only jumper left, I could move the bar up as I pleased, hitting critical milestone heights along the way. I moved the bar to six feet even, then to six feet, two inches, clearing both on the first tries.

Looking to Coach Page for advice, I said, "Coach, where do I go for the next height?"

Instead of giving me one height, he gave me two. "First, go to six feet, three and one-quarter inches and then go get your Olympic standard," he said with a bold confidence. Once again, his faith in me caused me to think beyond small goals and push further to the real prize. By telling me the next two heights rather than just one, he relayed an unspoken message to me.

He may have been yelling numbers and heights, but what I heard was, *Chaunté, I believe in you. It's not a matter of if you clear this next height, but when you clear this next height; then I want you to go claim your Olympic standard.*

I got the message loud and clear. After talking to the officials, they raised the bar to what was my current personal best. I stood at my mark, focused on the bar, and cleared the height by a mile. I didn't take time to celebrate; I knew the work was not done yet. Looking at the official, I smirked.

Getting my attention, he said, "Chaunté, where would you like us to put the bar?"

"I want the Olympic standard." As they raised the standard and reset the bar, I went back to my mark and, once again, stared at the bar. With confidence and grace, I ran toward the bar and once again cleared it. While I was still in the air, I let out a shrill scream. "Yes, it's done!" I knew I had just punched my ticket to the Olympic Trials and that I had a realistic shot of making the Olympic team.

The following two months seemed to go by at a world-record pace. Coach Page and I made last-minute preparations, but most of the hard work was already done.

16

OLYMPIC TRIALS

SIXTEEN YEARS AFTER watching the Olympics for the first time, I found myself in Sacramento, California, on a hot rubber track, attempting to make myself an Olympian. The rules for team selection were simple. The top twenty-five jumpers in the United States would all come here to battle for spots on the team. The top three finishers in this competition would represent Team USA as Olympians in Athens, Greece, as long as they had the qualifying standard. Having checked off the first box a few weeks ago, all that was left to do was get top three.

The battle would take place over two days, in two separate competitions with two days' rest in between. The first day would serve as an elimination session to cut the field's size by half.

Before taking the field, I stopped to talk to Coach Page. "Okay, Chaunté, you only need to clear three heights today. I've looked at the performance list, and not many women can jump higher than six feet, two inches. If you do that, you should easily make it to the second day of competition," he said before patting me on the back and sending me out to the field.

He was right. This round was simple. Clearing only three heights, I easily became one of the top fourteen finishers, qualifying for the high-jump final.

I felt calm and composed until that moment, but being so close to my life-changing goal caused me to feel anxious. Coach Page did his best to calm me, but I needed the comfort of the ones who had raised me. Once back at the hotel, I realized I needed to call my grandma. Picking up my silver flip phone, I dialed Grandma Bea's number and waited for her to answer.

"Hey, Grandma, I made it through to the final!" I said, trying to break the ice.

"I knew you would, but how are you feeling?" she said, careful not to create nerves if there were none.

"Grandma, what if I don't make it?" I said, deciding to confess my mounting fears.

"Chaunté, you have been preparing for this your whole life. You have done everything that you could do for this moment, and you are ready," my grandma affirmed.

"Grandma, I think that I need you here with me," I blurted out, showing her the full scale of my vulnerability.

"Chaunté, I don't have the money to get there, but I am going to try my best," she said. "If I can't make it, know that you can do it. You're going to have to put everything else out of your mind and accomplish what you went there to accomplish. Whether I make it or not, in two days, you will be an Olympian."

Somehow her words penetrated my worry and brought me comfort. She was right. I had done everything possible to prepare, and I was ready. The following two days, I stayed in my hotel room, shutting myself out from the world. I didn't think about the track meet because I learned a long time ago that obsessing over the details in the days leading up to a meet left me mentally exhausted and unable to perform. Instead, I read, played sudoku, and had random dance parties alone in my room. These distractions seemed to work, because I woke up feeling refreshed and at ease on the day of the competition.

At exactly 2:00 p.m., Coach Page arrived at the front of my hotel to pick me up. After strapping myself into the seat, I sat stoic and quiet as my nerves tried to get the best of me.

"So, what do you want to eat?" Coach said, trying his best to make me talk.

"I'm not hungry. I had a big breakfast," I said, trying to hide my mounting nausea.

"You have to eat something. This competition will go longer than you're used to, and you must fuel up," he persisted.

"Okay, can we go to Subway and get a sandwich?" I asked, hoping that would suffice.

"That works," he said gleefully, having won the battle.

On the way to lunch, Coach Page tried to keep me calm by telling me funny stories. I wanted to laugh but couldn't, so instead, I made conversation of my own. "Where's Tisha?" I asked, sincerely curious of her whereabouts.

Tisha Waller was also trained by Coach Page, and was one of the main reasons I trusted him to get me to the Olympics. She was an amazing jumper and one of the women who I would be competing with tonight. She had the best shot of making this Olympic team and had already represented the United States in the 1996 Olympic Games. I had been a fan of hers and was honored that we shared the same coach.

"She's going to meet us at the track," he said before parking in front of the sandwich shop. I went in and ordered my lunch but still found it hard to eat. Knowing the importance of this meal, I pushed through and ate anyway. Just as I was finishing, we arrived at the stadium. After parking, we walked to the warm-up track and found a place in the shade to sit down.

When it was almost time to go out and compete, I began my warm-up while pushing all my worries out of my head.

Still nervous, I searched for my grandma's face every five minutes, hoping that she'd made it. Once finished, I realized that she wasn't coming, and I would have to face this battle alone.

Settling my mind, I knew comforting words from her would have to be enough, and so I took out my cell phone and called my grandma's apartment. Her answering machine picked up. Choosing not to leave a message, I hung up, disappointed that I wouldn't be able to talk to her before I jumped.

Thinking quickly, I called another number that I knew would bring me comfort and calm before entering the biggest battle of my life.

Dialing my Uncle Joe's number, I pressed *Send* and waited for the other end of the receiver to pick up. Uncle Joe was my grandma's big brother and had also been my pastor at our church in Riverside. I'd kept in touch with him when I went to college and would often call him before big meets to pray for me. Even though I liked when he prayed for me, I loved when his wife, Aunt Bea, answered the phone. My uncle was humble and would always pray that God's will would be done no matter what the outcome. Aunt Bea, on the other hand, was more like me, having a warrior's mindset. Every time she prayed, she would ask, "God bless my grandniece and let her win this competition by a mile."

After two rings, I heard my uncle's voice on the other end of the line. "Hi, Uncle Joe," I said quickly, knowing that I would have to leave soon. "I'm in the warm-up track about to compete for my spot on the Olympic team, and I need you to pray for me," I pleaded with desperation in my voice.

Agreeing, he wasted no time and jumped right in. "Dear God, thank you for this moment. Would you please calm Chaunté's fears? Please let your will be done and help her see that she belongs here, and this moment has been your will for her life all along. May she fly on the wings of eagles and soar high above the bar until she makes this team. In your mighty name, we pray. Amen."

That prayer was perfect. I felt calm and at peace and was ready to compete. Just as he began to ask if my grandmother had made it, I heard the loudspeaker say, "Last call, women's high jump."

"Sorry, I have to go, Uncle Joe," I blurted out as I promptly hung up the phone and ran to the check-in tent.

Once we got onto the field, we measured our approaches and marked them with tape. Soon, we were called to line up across the infield. The crowd harnessed an electricity that I had never experienced at a track meet before. As I looked up into the crowd, I saw throngs of wildly cheering fans filling every seat in the stadium. Above the stands were suites, where VIP sponsors and honored guests watched the competition while eating fancy foods and being served refreshing drinks. Cameramen and women moved freely, flashing bright lights in our faces and trying their best to use photography to capture the gravity of this moment.

All fourteen of us women high-jump finalists lined up side by side, facing the crowd. The announcer began to introduce us over the loudspeaker one by one. Since I was toward the end of the lineup, I learned what to expect for my turn. After stating the athlete's affiliation, whether it was a school, track club, or major shoe sponsor, the announcer would run down a long list of the athlete's most impressive accomplishments. The speaker would then state the athlete's name, and as a grand finale, would pause, making way for their fans' thunderous cheers.

This process repeated itself for each competitor until it was my turn. Still unable to give up searching for my grandma, I scoured the crowd, trying to find her face. Among the thousands of people cheering, screaming, and jumping up and down, I quickly became discouraged.

Tuning back in to the announcer, I heard the last two introductions before my turn.

"Representing Asics, two-time Olympian, High School and Collegiate National Record Holder: Amy Acuff," the announcer said as my heart began to race. Amy's introduction sent the crowd into a cheering frenzy. Her family, friends, and fans appeared to have shown up for this event by the truckload. They were loud and excited to see her jump.

Next, they introduced my training partner. "Next in the order, representing Nike, we have the 1996 Olympian, World Championship Medalist, the indoor American record holder, Tisha Waller." Her family went crazy, also offering up a large and thunderous ovation.

After quickly being able to pinpoint her family by their cheering, I got an idea. If my grandma was here, maybe she would identify herself by cheering loudly and wildly after my introduction. Just as I'd finished my thought, the announcer began.

"Jumping next in the order, representing Georgia Tech, two-time NCAA Champion, Chaunté Howard."

Unlike the other jumpers, my applause was calm and tapered. I did not hear the loud solitary voice that I was looking for and realized that it was time to give up searching for my grandma.

"Okay, Chaunté. It's time to get ready to do what you came here to do," I said aloud to myself, knowing the importance of not dwelling on what I thought I needed but instead fighting hard for what I wanted. Today's goal was becoming an Olympian, and no matter what, I was going to do just that.

The rules for today's battle were simple. All fourteen of us women would jump in order, getting three attempts at each height. After the entire field either made the height or completed all their attempts, the bar would be raised, and we would repeat the process, eliminating women as we went along. When only three women were left, we would have our US Olympic Team.

The first height of the competition was five feet, ten and one-half inches. This was usually the height I came in during a college competition, but most of the other girls were out by then. Having fourteen other women jumping with me at this height was a new experience. To my relief, I cleared this bar on the first attempt, along with most of the field.

Going into the second height of six feet and three-quarter inches, I was nervous that many other women were still in the competition. After calming my nerves, I was able to clear the height on my first attempt. Finally, I saw glimmers of struggle; several women needed multiple attempts to clear this bar.

"Okay, ladies, we're raising the bar," the official said, placing a traffic cone in front of the jumping mat to stop us from making practice jumps.

Still too early in the competition to start focusing on which place I was in, I counted how many competitors were left in the field. Going into the third height of six feet, two and one-quarter inches, the field of fourteen jumpers had dwindled to nine.

Looking down at my hand, I noticed my fingertips were trembling. I had never experienced a meet where many women were still jumping when the bar was this high. Typically, by this time, I would have won the competition and would be jumping alone.

When it was my turn to jump, I looked over to the scoreboard and saw a one by my name, indicating that I was currently in first place. Usually, this placement would bring me peace, but today it didn't hold much weight. Since six of us had cleared the first two bars on our first attempts, there was currently a six-way tie for first place. Knowing the only way to break this tie was to continue to make first-attempt clearances, I forced myself to remain calm.

Okay, Chaunté, you have to make this height to hang on to first place, I thought.

Placing my toes on my measured white tape, I breathed in deeply and took a giant step backward before powering forward toward the bar. Mid-stride, my spike snagged the track, causing me to stumble. With my momentum carrying me forward, I realized it was too late to abandon the jump. Planting my foot into the ground, I tried my best to propel over the bar.

Instead of sailing up and over the height, I crashed into the bar, causing it to tumble to the ground.

My heart sank. Turning to the scoreboard, I saw that my horror was confirmed. With that one miss, I had dropped from first down to sixth place. Hanging my head in shame, I couldn't believe I had let first place slip out of my hands so easily.

Running to the sidelines, I found Coach Page to get guidance on what adjustments I needed to make to clear the bar on my second attempt.

"Coach Page, what did I do wrong?" I asked, desperately in need of a solution.

"You just tripped. Replay the jump in your mind and try again. This time you will make it." He was right. I lined back up at my mark, jumped, and made it on my second try. We lost several women at this height before the officials closed the pit to raise the bar.

Only four women were left in the competition as we went into the fourth height of six feet, three and one-half inches. This should have been a relief because I had come so far, but it wasn't. My work was far from done. Out of the four women, I was currently in last place by misses. All three of the other competitors had cleared every other bar on the first try.

"All right, ladies, we are raising the bar to six feet, three and a half inches," the official said before closing the pit to practice jumps.

Now sizing up my competitors, I realized I was the only woman left in the competition who was not a professional. Standing five feet, eight inches tall, I was the shortest woman left in the fight, and it was clear that I was the underdog. Tisha, the indoor American record holder, stood six feet tall; Amy, the two-time Olympian, stood six feet, two inches tall; and Erin Aldrich, the professional volleyball player, stood six feet, three inches tall.

Just outside of medal contention, I knew I only had to beat one of these ladies to make the team, and I couldn't let my height disadvantage be my excuse for losing.

Feeling desperate to improve my place standing, I decided the best strategy to clear would be to run as fast as possible and hope to clear the bar.

Tisha and Amy both cleared the bar on the first attempt, keeping them tied for first. When it was my turn to jump, I began to execute the plan I had just constructed in my head.

Taking my mark, I ran as fast as I could, but when I tried to jump, the momentum that I generated caused me to sail straight into the bar. The bar once again toppled to the ground.

Realizing that I had left the door wide open for my defeat, I chastised myself. *Why would you abandon what you and Coach Page have been practicing all year? That was so dumb!*

My fate was now in Erin's hands. If she cleared this bar on her first attempt, I had almost no chance of medaling or making this team.

Knowing that my dream was slipping between my fingers, I felt tears begin to well up in my eyes, causing me to run to Coach Page for direction. "Coach, how can I fix this?" I said, wanting desperately to go back to the fundamentals that had gotten us to this moment.

"Chaunté, that was not what we practiced. Do what we've practiced, and you will be fine."

As he talked, I heard the crowd sigh in disappointment, causing me to look back at the high-jump pit. While Coach Page and I were devising a plan, Erin had taken her turn and missed the bar.

This is the break I needed, I said to myself before heading back to the infield. If I could clear this bar before her, I would be in third place and most likely make this team.

Taking my mark, I exhaled deeply to steady my breath. Forcing myself to relax, I ran toward the bar significantly more slowly than in my previous attempt. This proved to be an overcorrection because, once again, the bar fell to the ground.

Immediately, tears welled up and fell from my eyes. I'd messed up. Once again, I'd given Erin a perfect opportunity to beat me. If neither of us could clear this height, she would be the one going to Athens and not me.

Completely defeated, I realized that for whatever reason, I didn't have it tonight. I was not used to missing the bar and almost always cleared bars on the first attempt. Going back to my bag, I waited for Erin to jump. I started to sniffle, fighting back deep sobs as I prepared to take what could be my last jump of the competition.

For her second attempt, Erin ran up to the bar and jumped up high, getting her body over the bar. The crowd began to cheer, but then her foot tapped the bar off in a split second, causing the cheers to be cut short. The bar toppled to the ground, handing Erin her second miss.

My last chance of becoming an Olympian depended on me clearing this bar, but I didn't have the confidence that I could do it. Standing at my mark, I began to tremble as I waited for the officials to reset the bar. The crowd was silent as they waited to see the drama unfold. Trying my best to picture a perfect jump in my mind, I closed my eyes and began to visualize myself clearing the bar.

A solitary voice pierced the silence of the crowd and my thoughts. "I'm here, I'm here," I heard someone yell in the distance.

"Chaunté, I'm here."

Looking to the stands, I saw my grandma making her way down the stadium stairs, coming closer to the high-jump apron. "Chaunté, I'm here. You can do this!" she screamed. Making her way to the front row, she waved frantically, trying to get my attention. "Jump over the bar," she said as the last reassurance.

Realizing I'd seen her, she quieted, allowing me to concentrate.

Every bit of fear vanished, and I was overcome with joy. I was no longer alone. My tribe was there with me, and I felt empowered to do what I had come there to do. Adrenaline pumped through my body, preparing me for my last jump of the competition. Taking my mark, I stood behind my tape, leaned back, and bounded toward the bar. Comfort and speed radiated from every muscle in my body, and I soared high over the bar before landing effortlessly onto the mat. The crowd erupted.

The loudspeaker announced, "We have clearance for Chaunté Howard." Looking toward the scoreboard, I waited for my name to appear, and when it did, I saw a three by my name, indicating that I was in third place. Erin also attempted the height but was unable to clear it.

Jumping up in the air, I screamed. "Yes. I did it!" I looked over toward my grandma, who beamed as tears flowed from her eyes. I felt unstoppable. The bar was raised, and I cleared the next height of six feet, four and three-quarters inches, taking the silver medal.

Tisha, Amy, and I were called to the middle of the stadium for the medal presentation. Once we were all on top of our place platforms, the announcer said, "I now introduce to you your 2004 women's high jump Olympians."

Flashbacks to the first time I saw FloJo race out of the blocks flooded my head. Examining my medal, I thought of the nights when I was homeless and hungry and how that girl dreamed of standing where I stood right now.

"Over here, Chaunté," said one of the many photographers as bright lights flashed in our faces. I would never say being separated from my mom and sisters was a blessing, but now it seemed like part of a bigger plan. I became strong and resilient. I learned how to fight through pain and disappointment. When things got tough, I learned how to will my way through, and when I was at my weakest, I knew I could depend on the strength of those who loved me. I never spent a lot of time focusing on the people who were not there for me but appreciated those who were. That day, my grandma came through for me in a big way, and if she hadn't, I don't know if I would have had the strength to make it over the bronze-medal height.

When the bright lights stopped flashing, I broke away from the crowd and ran over to my grandma and gave her a big hug and kiss. "We did it, Grandma," I said, holding up my medal to provide her with a better look.

"No, Chaunté, you did it, and now, forever, you will be known as a United States Olympian."

Newborn baby Chaunté in the arms of her mother, Natalie Jackson, with sisters Tania (upper right) and Alexis (lower right) in 1984.

Family Christmas gathering, 1992, from left to right: Grandma Beatrice Jackson, Aunt Debbie Harris (who took Chaunté in years later), older cousin Sarah Jackson, sister Alexis Howard, Chaunté, younger cousin Candace Harris.

Chaunté (center right) with friend Tracee Thomas (center left) in her freshman year of high school at J. W. North High in Riverside, California, 1999.

Chaunté (rear, standing) with middle school best friends Taiyana Harrison (left) and Toshiona Bradley (right), 1987.

Chaunté at the state championships in Long Beach, California, 2000.

Chaunté running the relay at state championships, Long Beach, California, 2001.

Chaunté with her grandmother Beatrice Jackson in 2002.

Chaunté receiving senior track awards at the Mission Inn Hotel, Riverside, California, before graduating from high school in 2002.

Chaunté attending her high school graduation celebration at Riverside Faith Temple church in 2002.

Posing with meet officials after winning the 2003 Penn Relay Championships at historic Franklin Field in Philadelphia.

Chaunté approaching the high jump bar at a 2003 home meet at Georgia Tech (Georgia Institute of Technology).

Chaunté clearing the bar, 2003.

Chaunté breaking the school record as a freshman at Georgia Tech in 2003.

Chaunté wins the gold medal at her first Atlantic Coast Conference championship at Clemson University in 2003.

Chaunté's first visit home from college for Christmas 2003, pictured with Grandma Beatrice Jackson.

On the same visit, Chaunté with her mother, Natalie Jackson, 2003.

Chaunté at the warm-up track at the 2008 Beijing Olympics, just before taking the field to jump in the famous Bird's Nest stadium.

Coach Nathaniel Page, with Chaunté in the background, 2008.

Chaunté jumping in her first professional indoor competition, 2006.

Chaunté sets up to clear the high jump bar (above) and soars over it (below) in 2004 at Georgia Tech.

Chaunté lands a long jump at Georgia Tech in 2004.

ACKNOWLEDGMENTS

Thank you, Lisa Sandell, for giving my story a voice. I have wanted to write this book for so long. You believed in me, took the project on, and made it happen. This book would have never become a reality if it were not for your vision and your expertise.

To the entire Scholastic team. Thank you for providing a window into the wide world through books for children trapped behind the walls of limited resources! You always have been and will always be my heroes!